Intro

ACTIVE
Skills for Communication

Chuck Sandy • Curtis Kelly

Series Consultant:
Neil J. Anderson

2·17

HEINLE
CENGAGE Learning

Australia • Brazil • Japan • Korea • Mexico • Singapore • Spain • United Kingdom • United States

HEINLE
CENGAGE Learning™

ACTIVE Skills for Communication,
Intro Student Book
Sandy / Kelly / Anderson

Publisher: Andrew Robinson

Editorial Manager: Sean Bermingham

Senior Development Editor: Ian Purdon

Associate Development Editor:
Lauren Rodan

Director of Global Marketing: Ian Martin

Content Project Manager: Tan Jin Hock

Senior Print Buyer: Mary Beth Hennebury

Editorial and Production Project Management:
Content*Ed Publishing Solutions, LLC

Illustrator: Raketshop Design Studio

Compositor: Chrome Media Group / C. Hanzie

Cover Designer: Chrome Media Group /
M. Chong / C. Hanzie

Cover Images: All photos from Shutterstock,
except bottom (Photos.com)

Photo Credits

iStockphoto: pages 13 (top left), 14, 15, 19
(bottom right), 39, 67, 123 (top row); Photos.
com: pages 13 (bottom left), 21 (bottom right
three photos), 24 (second from left), 45 (second
row right), 47 (far left, center left, center right),
52 (far left and center left), 54 (top right, second
row all, third row right, bottom row center),
56 (top right), 58 (top right and center left),
61, 67 (far left, second from left, far right, and
second from right), 70, 71, 78, 79, 81, 86 (bottom
right), 88 (top right and bottom left), 112 (far
left and center) 114; Shutterstock: pages 18, 19
(all except bottom right), 24 (far left, far right,
and second from right), 27 (center and right),
31, 32, 34, 38 (all except center right), 41, 44, 45
(top row and second row left), 47 (far right), 50,
51, 52 (far right and center right), 54 (top left),
56 (bottom), 58 (all except top right and center
left), 60, 66, 72, 74, 75, 86 (all except bottom
right), 88 (top left and center and bottom right),
112 (all except far left and center), 113, 121, 122
(top row center), 123 (bottom); Index Open:
pages 24 (center), 27 (left), 38 (center right), 45
(bottom), 54 (third row left, bottom left, and
bottom right), 56 (top left and center); Landov:
page 122 (top left, top right, and bottom right)

For permission to use material from this text or product,
submit all requests online at **www.cengage.com/permissions**
Further permissions questions can be emailed to
permissionrequest@cengage.com

Student Book ISBN-13: 978-1-4130-2034-2
Student Book ISBN-10: 1-4130-2034-8
Book + Student Audio CD ISBN-13: 978-1-4240-0905-3
Book + Student Audio CD ISBN-10: 1-4240-0905-7

Heinle
20 Channel Center Street
Boston, Massachusetts 02210
USA

Cengage Learning is a leading provider of customized learning solutions with office
locations around the globe, including Singapore, the United Kingdom, Australia, Mexico,
Brazil, and Japan. Locate our local office at:
international.cengage.com/region

Cengage Learning products are represented in Canada by Nelson Education, Ltd.

Visit Heinle online at **elt.heinle.com**
Visit our corporate website at **www.cengage.com**

Printed in Canada
4 5 6 7 8 9 10   13 12 11 10

DEDICATION AND ACKNOWLEDGMENTS

This book is dedicated to our families who have patiently endured our long periods of writing, and who have helped so much along the way with comments, suggestions, love, and support. We'd also like to dedicate this book to our students over the years for bearing with us as we tried out early versions of the activities that became *ACTIVE Skills for Communication*. By teaching us what learning is, they helped shape the ideas from which this course has arisen. Thanks go, too, to our editors at Cengage Learning, who have supported this project from the time it was first proposed several years ago. Their belief in our approach and vision for the course has been an enormous blessing. Particular thanks go to Chris Sol Cruz, who first embraced the idea of *ACTIVE Skills for Communication*, Sean Bermingham and Guy De Villiers, who helped shape our approach, and Ian Purdon, who tirelessly worked with us through each and every page of the many versions of each unit. We could not have done it without you.

Our hope is that teachers around the world can use this series as a way to engage and motivate their learners, and that their students will be as successful in doing the activities and as enriched by them as our students have been.

We appreciate enormously the input we received from students and teachers in Korea, Thailand, Taiwan, Japan, Brazil, and the United States, including Oral Communication students at Osaka Gakuin and Heian Jogakuin Universities, and Oral Strategies students at Chubu University. We would especially like to thank Dr. Yoshiyasu Shirai, Anne Shirai, Daryl Aragaki, and Rex Tanimoto at Osaka Gakuin University.

Chuck Sandy & Curtis Kelly

Reviewers

Daryl Aragaki, Osaka Gakuin University; **Mayumi Asaba**, Osaka Gakuin University; **Rima Bahous**, Lebanese American University; **Phillip Barkman**, Asia University; **Edmar da Silva Falcão**, CEI—Centro De Ensino De Idioma; **Muriel Fujii**, Osaka Gakuin University; **Arlen Gargagliano**, writer; **John Gebhardt**, Thailand; **Chris Hammond**, Kyoto Gakuen University; **Ann-Marie Hadzima**, National Taiwan University; **Brian Heldenbrand**, Jeonju University; **Caroline C. Hwang**, National Taipei University of Technology; **Mitsuyo Ito**, Osaka Gakuin University; **Hiroshi Izumi**, Tomigaoka Super English High School; **Kirsten Johannsen**, ELT specialist, the United States; **Leina Jucá**, MAI English; **Steve Jugovich**, Seikei Sports University; **Yuco Kikuchi**, English Pier School owner; **Michelle Misook Kim**, Kyung Hee University; **Kevin Knight**, Kanda University of International Studies; **Sumie Kudo**, Osaka Gakuin; **Thamana Lekprichakul**, Kyoto University, Sogo Chikyu Kankyogaku Kenkyujo; **Hae Chin Moon**, Korea University; **Adam Murray**, Tokyo Denki University; **Heidi Nachi**, Ritsumeikan University; **Miho Omori**, Keirinkan; **Bill Pellowe**, Kinki University; **Nigel Randell**, Ryukoku University; **Alex Rath**, Shih Hsin University; **Gregg Schroeder**, ELT specialist, Hong Kong; **Pornpimol Senawong**, Silpakorn University; **Jeffrey Shaffer**, Shimane University; **Kyoko Shirakata**, ELT specialist; **Masahiro Shirai**, Doshisha Girls' Junior and Senior High Schools; **Thang Siew Ming**, Universiti Kebangsaan Malaysia; **Stephen Slater**, ELT specialist; **Wang Songmei**, Beijing Institute of Education; **Scott Smith**, Kansai Gaidai University; **Joe Spear**, Hanbat National University; **Bernard Susser**, Doshisha Women's University; **Rex Tanimoto**, Osaka Gakuin University; **Ellen Tanoura**, Osaka Gakuin University; **Dave Tonetti**, Kyung Hee University; **Yoko Wakui**, Aoyama Gakuin Junior College, Keisei University; **Matthew Walsh**, Momoyama Gakuin High School and Ikeda High School; **James Webb**, Kansai Gaidai University; **Nancy Yu**, ELT specialist; **Dorothy Zemach**, writer

SCOPE AND SEQUENCE

Unit	Challenge	Skills	Fluency	Language
1. Personal Poster *Page 12*	Creating self-introduction poster and talking about it	Greeting people; Sharing personal information	Agreeing and disagreeing *I think so too.*	**Descriptions** She looks athletic. **Wh- questions & answers** What's this? / What are these? / Who's this? **Adding more information** She's my best friend.
2. Our Favorites *Page 18*	Interviewing other students and finding out who likes the same things	Talking about likes and dislikes; Guessing information	Comparing opinions *How about you?*	**Like/dislike verbs** crazy about, love, like, it's OK, hate, can't stand **Yes/No questions & answers with** *do* Do you like karaoke? Yes, I do. **Talking about favorites** flavor, color, sport, food, music, movie
3. Design a Town *Page 24*	Designing an ideal town, explaining the layout to a partner, and drawing your partner's town	Describing locations	Confirming information *Across from the pizza place?*	**Geographic features & buildings** mountains, house, fitness center, park ***There is . . . & There are . . .*** **Prepositions of place** in front of, across from, next to
Project 1. Neighborhood Walking Tour *Page 30*	**Recycling themes and language from Unit 3** Drawing simple maps of walking tours and presenting them to other students			
4. What's for Dinner? *Page 32*	Comparing grocery items to find out what someone is making for dinner	Talking about food	Interrupting *Excuse me.*	**Food words** tomatoes, fruit, rice, peaches **Questions & answers with** *How many are there?* How many melons are there? There are two. Is there any garlic? Yes, there's some garlic. **Containers & packaging** a bag of spaghetti, a bottle of cooking oil
5. Every Day's a Holiday *Page 38*	Designing an original holiday and describing it to classmates	Explaining daily and holiday routines	Using pause fillers *Hmm . . .*	**Frequency adverbs** always, usually, sometimes, never **Special days** the last day of school, Valentine's Day **Holiday activities** On Christmas we exchange presents.
6. The Everyday Hero Award *Page 44*	Making an award for a special person and telling other students about it	Describing people and showing appreciation	Evaluating what you hear *That sounds fun!*	**Jobs** cook, bus driver **Yes/No questions & answers with** *is, do/does* Is he the school guard? Yes, he is. Does he work at the front gate? Yes, he does. **Description words** He's so thoughtful. She's really nice.
Project 2. Who's Who Around School *Page 50*	**Recycling themes and language from Unit 6** Interviewing someone at school, making an information page about that person, and introducing the person to the class			

Unit	Challenge	Skills	Fluency	Language
7. Now Hiring *Page 52*	Designing an original job and describing it to other students	Asking about job requirements	Showing surprise *Are you kidding?*	**Job routines** Serve food. Put the things they buy in bags. ***Have to* for actions** What do I have to do? You have to wear a uniform. **More jobs** mail carrier, English teacher
8. Family Ties *Page 58*	Discussing the information and photos in a family tree to identify each person	Describing family members	Clarifying *Please say that again.*	**Family relationships** She's my cousin. He's Bob's uncle. **Asking about & describing people** Who's this? She's my aunt. **Adding more information** She's married with two children.
9. Timeline *Page 64*	Making a timeline of major life events and asking questions about events in other students' lives	Describing past events and experiences	Showing concern *Were you scared?*	**Major life events & time expressions** When I was a child, I got an award. **Simple past for experiences** I went to Spain. I bought a guitar. **Emotions** proud, bored, worried
Project 3. Mini Scrapbook *Page 70*	**Recycling themes and language from Unit 9** Making a one-page scrapbook of a big life event and telling other students about it			
10. An Amazing Trip *Page 72*	Designing a three-day tour and explaining the activities to other students	Talking about plans	Showing you are listening *Uh-huh.*	**Vacation options** A homestay on a ranch in Texas **Simple future to describe plans** First, you'll go to a castle. **Money** I'll use $50 to go sightseeing.
11. Computer Dating Service *Page 78*	Interviewing a classmate and finding an ideal partner for him or her	Describing personalities and personal preferences	Asking for specific details *Like what, for example?*	**Character traits and activity preferences** He talks a lot. I like outdoor activities. ***Who* relative clauses** I like people who are interested in sports. ***Like* + infinitive** Are you someone who likes to stay at home or to go out? I like to go out.
12. Talent Show *Page 84*	Showing classmates a special talent or skill, telling them about it, and teaching them how to do it	Giving instructions	Checking instructions *Like this?*	**Special talents** Do a card trick. Play an instrument. **Imperatives for instructions** Do this with your fingers. **Order words** first, now, then
Project 4. Personal Progress Bookmark *Page 90*	**Evaluating progress and successes from Intro Student Book** Making bookmarks that show progress and presenting self-assessments to the class			

WELCOME!

To learners:

Welcome to *ACTIVE Skills for Communication*. Here are some suggestions to help you get as much as possible from this course.

- First, be active. Make using and learning English your personal goal. Be active in learning English by being active in using it.
- Second, don't be afraid to make mistakes. Each mistake is a step toward learning.
- Third, be aware of how communication involves critical thinking and decision making. This thinking is an important part of learning.
- Fourth, develop learning strategies. Decide what you need to learn. Then find the ways to learn that best fit your style.
- Fifth, learn how the different parts of a unit work, so that you can get the most out of them.
- In short, be positive toward communicating in English. There are many new experiences waiting for you in the pages that follow.

Chuck Sandy & Curtis Kelly

To teachers:

What are the basic characteristics of this course?

First, it is goal-oriented. Each unit builds toward a final speaking activity, such as an interview, a presentation, a game, a role-play, or a discussion. These *Challenge* activities are more than straightforward language exercises—they foster meaningful interaction between students and are based on real situations language learners face both inside and outside of the classroom.

Second, it is strategy-oriented. Interacting in English requires a greater repertoire of skills than just being able to produce the right grammar and vocabulary. It requires learners to identify goals, choose strategies, speak expressively, and respond appropriately. Learners are encouraged to think critically about the language they are learning, thereby helping them integrate communication strategies into real interactions.

Finally, it makes learners active. Personalized speaking activities throughout the course give learners ownership of their interactions and their learning. When students use English to relate real experiences, frame real opinions, and respond genuinely to others, English becomes more than something to study. It becomes something to broaden their perspectives.

ARE YOU AN *ACTIVE* COMMUNICATOR?

Before you use this book to develop your communication skills, think about your speaking and listening habits, and your strengths and weaknesses when communicating in English. Check [✔] the statements that are true for you.

1. I look for chances to use English.
   ☐ Start of course   ☐ End of course

2. I sometimes speak English with people who speak my first language.
   ☐ Start of course   ☐ End of course

3. I enjoy communicating in English with English speakers.
   ☐ Start of course   ☐ End of course

4. I think communicating in English is fun.
   ☐ Start of course   ☐ End of course

5. I tell myself, "Speaking English is easy."
   ☐ Start of course   ☐ End of course

6. I don't mind making pronunciation, vocabulary, or grammar mistakes.
   ☐ Start of course   ☐ End of course

7. If the listener does not understand something, I try to say it in a different way.
   ☐ Start of course   ☐ End of course

8. I listen to how other people say things in English, such as in movies or music.
   ☐ Start of course   ☐ End of course

9. When I listen, I try to get the message rather than try to understand every word.
   ☐ Start of course   ☐ End of course

10. If I can't understand what someone is saying very well, I guess.
    ☐ Start of course   ☐ End of course

11. I'm a good listener—I listen carefully to what other people are saying.
    ☐ Start of course   ☐ End of course

12. I don't answer questions with just one word, such as "yes" or "no." I say more.
    ☐ Start of course   ☐ End of course

13. I try to think in English before speaking, rather than translate from my language.
    ☐ Start of course   ☐ End of course

14. I participate in class, talking as much as I can.
    ☐ Start of course   ☐ End of course

15. I sometimes review what we study in class at home.
    ☐ Start of course   ☐ End of course

16. I plan to travel to an English-speaking country if I can.
    ☐ Start of course   ☐ End of course

At the end of the course, answer the quiz again to see if you have become a more fluent, active communicator.

Personal Poster 1

Challenge Preview

Unit Challenge
▸ Make a poster about yourself.
▸ Use it to introduce yourself.

A Write. Complete the chart with your details.

Reynaldo Diaz

First name:
Reynaldo

Last name:
Diaz

Nickname:
Rey

Yumi Ito

First name:
Yumi

Last name:
Ito

Nickname:
none

You:

First name:

Last name:

Nickname:

B Write and listen. Reynaldo and Yumi are doing the *Challenge* at the end of this unit. Yumi is explaining her poster. Write *you* or *me* to complete the conversation. Then listen to check your answers.

Rey: Hi. I'm Reynaldo Diaz.

Yumi: Hi, Reynaldo. I'm Yumi Ito.

Rey: It's nice to meet _____.
Please call _____ Rey.

Yumi: Call me Yumi. All my friends do.

Rey: OK, Yumi. Please tell _____ about your poster. What's this?

Yumi: It's my hometown. I'm from Tokyo.

C Speak. Now practice the conversation with a partner. Then change the words in red to talk about yourself.

1. Each unit begins with the *Challenge Preview*. The warm-up pictures at the top get you thinking about the unit topic and the dialog at the bottom gets you thinking about the *Challenge*—that's the big speaking activity at the end of the unit. The dialog is from two students doing the *Challenge*. Listening to them and practicing yourself helps you prepare to do the *Challenge*.

2. *Working on Language* teaches you some of the basic language you'll need in this unit. The box at the top shows some important language points and the exercises under it help you learn them. Remember: Each page builds towards the *Challenge*.

Working on Language ▸ Explaining Your Poster

Question	Answer	More Information
What's this?	It's the Great Wall.	It's very long.
What are these?	They're DVDs.	I have 200!
Who's this?	She's my sister.	She's my best friend.

A Match and number. Look at the examples in the box. Draw lines to match the questions and answers. Then number the pictures.

1. What's this? • • They're telephones. • • I can see it from my house.
2. What are these? • • It's Taipei 101. • • Someday, I want to go there.
3. What's this? • • He's my math teacher. • • I get a lot of phone calls.
4. Who's this? • • It's a map of Australia. • • I love his class.

B Write and speak. Complete the conversations. Add one more conversation with your own information. Then practice with a partner.

1.

A: _____ this?
B: _____ an MP3 player. I love music.
A: Me too!

2.

A: _____ this?
B: _____ my best friend. He's a student.
A: He's cute!

3.

A: _____ these?
B: _____ textbooks. I study English.
A: That's interesting.

Level Up!
See page 112.

4.
Your Idea!

A: _____
B: _____
_____
A: _____

3. *Communicate* lets you use the language you just learned. It also gives you a chance to talk with your classmates about interesting things and helps you prepare for the *Challenge* at the same time.

  * Note to teacher: The end of this page is a great place to stop if you are teaching the unit in two lessons.

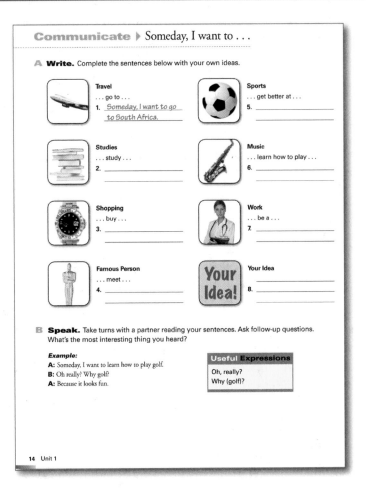

Communicate ▶ Someday, I want to . . .

A Write. Complete the sentences below with your own ideas.

Travel
. . . go to . . .
1. _Someday, I want to go to South Africa._

Sports
. . . get better at . . .
5. _____

Studies
. . . study . . .
2. _____

Music
. . . learn how to play . . .
6. _____

Shopping
. . . buy . . .
3. _____

Work
. . . be a . . .
7. _____

Famous Person
. . . meet . . .
4. _____

Your Idea
8. _____

B Speak. Take turns with a partner reading your sentences. Ask follow-up questions. What's the most interesting thing you heard?

Example:
A: Someday, I want to learn how to play golf.
B: Oh really? Why golf?
A: Because it looks fun.

Useful Expressions
Oh, really?
Why (golf)?

14   Unit 1

Working on Fluency ▶ Agreeing and Disagreeing

A 🔊 **Listen.** Cathy and Sarah are talking about their classmates. Draw lines to match each person with the descriptions.

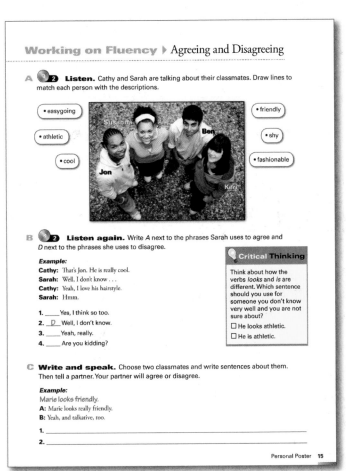

• easygoing

• athletic

• cool

• friendly

• shy

• fashionable

B 🔊 **Listen again.** Write *A* next to the phrases Sarah uses to agree and *D* next to the phrases she uses to disagree.

Example:
Cathy: That's Jon. He is really cool.
Sarah: Well, I don't know . . .
Cathy: Yeah, I love his hairstyle.
Sarah: Hmm.

1. _____ Yes, I think so too.
2. _D_ Well, I don't know.
3. _____ Yeah, really.
4. _____ Are you kidding?

Critical Thinking

Think about how the verbs *looks* and *is* are different. Which sentence should you use for someone you don't know very well and you are not sure about?
☐ He looks athletic.
☐ He is athletic.

C Write and speak. Choose two classmates and write sentences about them. Then tell a partner. Your partner will agree or disagree.

Example:
Marie looks friendly.
A: Marie looks really friendly.
B: Yeah, and talkative, too.

1. _____
2. _____

Personal Poster   15

4. *Working on Fluency* gives you useful tools for conversations. You can learn how to respond to things people say, ask for more information, check what you hear, interrupt, and do other things to make your conversations smoother. The conversations on the CD let you listen to speakers using these techniques. The exercises let you practice using the techniques yourself.

5. The *Challenge* is the big speaking activity at the end of the unit. The *Challenge* lets you communicate with other students in English, using the language and skills you learned in the unit. The *Challenges* include games, interviews, role-plays, and other activities. The *Challenges* let you use English to share ideas, make things, and get to know your classmates better.

When doing the *Challenge*, don't worry about using perfect English, but try to do it all in English. The *Challenge* gets you to use everything you learned to really communicate with your classmates.

Reflection Time lets you review your progress and write down the new language you learned.

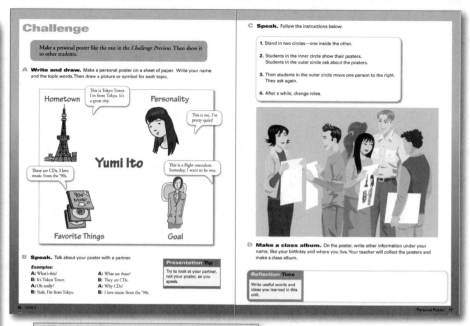

6. Try the fun *When You Have Time* and *Level Up* activities at the back of the book when you finish an activity before your classmates. Some can be done alone, and others must be done with a partner.

7. The *Projects* take learning beyond the classroom. You'll prepare a personal project outside of class and present it to your classmates. Each project will give you the chance to express yourself.

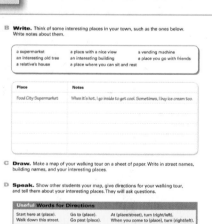

CLASSROOM LANGUAGE

Language you can hear in the class:

Open your books to Unit 1.

Listen to the conversation.

Compare answers with a partner.

Find a partner.

Let's do part A.

Look at the *Warm-up* page.

Make groups of four.

Work by yourself.

Language you can use in class:

Please say that again.

Did you say (page 12)?

What does _____ mean?

How do you say _____ in English?

Reynaldo

Kirsten

I don't understand. Please explain again.

We're finished.

James

Sang-mi

What should we do next?

How do you spell that?

Language you can use to work with a partner or in a group:

Can I go first?

What do you think?

It's your turn.

How about you?

Yumi

That's a good idea!

That's interesting. Thanks.

Ethan

Personal Poster 1

Challenge Preview

Unit Challenge
- ▸ Make a poster about yourself.
- ▸ Use it to introduce yourself.

A **Write.** Complete the chart with your details.

Reynaldo Diaz

First name:
Reynaldo

Last name:
Diaz

Nickname:
Rey

Yumi Ito

First name:
Yumi

Last name:
Ito

Nickname:
none

You:

First name:

Last name:

Nickname:

B **1** **Write and listen.** Reynaldo and Yumi are doing the *Challenge* at the end of this unit. Yumi is explaining her poster. Write *you* or *me* to complete the conversation. Then listen to check your answers.

Rey: Hi. I'm **Reynaldo Diaz**.

Yumi: Hi, **Reynaldo**. I'm **Yumi Ito**.

Rey: It's nice to meet _____.

Please, call _____ **Rey**.

Yumi: Call me **Yumi**. All my friends do.

Rey: OK, **Yumi**. Please tell _____ about your poster. What's this?

Yumi: It's my hometown. I'm from **Tokyo**.

C **Speak.** Now practice the conversation with a partner. Then change the words in red to talk about yourself.

Working on Language ▶ Explaining Your Poster

Question	Answer	More Information
What's this?	It's the Great Wall.	It's very long.
What are these?	They're DVDs.	I have 200!
Who's this?	She's my sister.	She's my best friend.

A **Match and number.** Look at the examples in the box. Draw lines to match the questions and answers. Then number the pictures.

1. What's this? •
•They're telephones. •
• I can see it from my house.

2. What are these? •
•It's Taipei 101. •
• Someday, I want to go there.

3. What's this? •
• He's my math teacher. •
• I get a lot of phone calls.

4. Who's this? •
• It's a map of Australia. •
• I love his class.

B **Write and speak.** Complete the conversations. Add one more conversation with your own information. Then practice with a partner.

1.

A: _____ this?

B: _____ an MP3 player. I love music.

A: Me too!

3.

A: _____ these?

B: _____ textbooks. I study English.

A: That's interesting.

> **Level Up!**
> See page 112.

2.

A: _____ this?

B: _____ my best friend. He's a student.

A: He's cute!

4. Your Idea!

A: _____

B: _____

_____

A: _____

Communicate ▶ Someday, I want to . . .

A Write. Complete the sentences below with your own ideas.

 **Travel**
. . . go to . . .
1. Someday, I want to go to South Africa.

 **Sports**
. . . get better at . . .
5. _____

 **Studies**
. . . study . . .
2. _____

 **Music**
. . . learn how to play . . .
6. _____

 **Shopping**
. . . buy . . .
3. _____

 **Work**
. . . be a . . .
7. _____

 **Famous Person**
. . . meet . . .
4. _____

Your Idea! **Your Idea**
8. _____

B Speak. Take turns with a partner reading your sentences. Ask follow-up questions. What's the most interesting thing you heard?

Example:
A: Someday, I want to learn how to play golf.
B: Oh really? Why golf?
A: Because it looks fun.

Useful Expressions
Oh, really?
Why (golf)?

Working on Fluency ▶ Agreeing and Disagreeing

A 🔘**2** **Listen.** Cathy and Sarah are talking about their classmates. Draw lines to match each person with the descriptions.

- easygoing
- athletic
- cool
- friendly
- shy
- fashionable

B 🔘**2** **Listen again.** Write *A* next to the phrases Sarah uses to agree and *D* next to the phrases she uses to disagree.

Example:
Cathy: That's Jon. He is really cool.
Sarah: Well, I don't know . . .
Cathy: Yeah, I love his hairstyle.
Sarah: Hmm.

1. _____ Yes, I think so too.
2. _D_ Well, I don't know.
3. _____ Yeah, really.
4. _____ Are you kidding?

> 💡 **Critical Thinking**
>
> Think about how the verbs *looks* and *is* are different. Which sentence should you use for someone you don't know very well and you are not sure about?
>
> ☐ He looks athletic.
> ☐ He is athletic.

C **Write and speak.** Choose two classmates and write sentences about them. Then tell a partner. Your partner will agree or disagree.

Example:
Marie looks friendly.
A: Marie looks really friendly.
B: Yeah, and talkative, too.

1. _____

2. _____

Challenge

Make a personal poster like the one in the *Challenge Preview.* Then show it to other students.

A **Write and draw.** Make a personal poster on a sheet of paper. Write your name and the topic words. Then draw a picture or symbol for each topic.

B **Speak.** Talk about your poster with a partner.

Examples:

A: What's this?
B: It's Tokyo Tower.
A: Oh really?
B: Yeah, I'm from Tokyo.

A: What are these?
B: They are CDs.
A: Why CDs?
B: I love music from the '90s.

Presentation Tip

Try to look at your partner, not your poster, as you speak.

C **Speak.** Follow the instructions below:

> **1.** Stand in two circles—one inside the other.
>
> **2.** Students in the inner circle show their posters.
> Students in the outer circle ask about the posters.
>
> **3.** Then students in the outer circle move one person to the right.
> They ask again.
>
> **4.** After a while, change roles.

D **Make a class album.** On the poster, write other information under your name, like your birthday and where you live. Your teacher will collect the posters and make a class album.

Reflection Time

Write useful words and ideas you learned in this unit.

2

Challenge Preview

Unit Challenge

▶ Interview other students.
▶ Find a student who likes the same things you do.

A Write. Do you like ice cream? Circle your favorite flavor.

strawberry   **green tea**   **chocolate**   **cherry**   **vanilla**

B 3 Write and listen. James and Kirsten are talking about ice cream. Write *?* or *!* at the end of the sentences to complete the conversation. Then listen to check your answers.

Kirsten:	Do you like ice cream___
James:	Yes, I do. I love it___ How about you___
Kirsten:	I like it too. What kind of ice cream do you like___
James:	Strawberry. It's my favorite. Do you like strawberry ice cream, too___
Kirsten:	No, I don't. I can't stand it___

C Speak. Now practice the conversation with a partner. Then change the words in red to talk about other ice cream flavors.

Working on Language ▶ Explaining Likes and Dislikes

Question	Answer	
Do you like karaoke?	Yes, I do. I'm **crazy about** it.	**Love**
	Yes. I **like** karaoke.	
	Karaoke is **OK**.	
	No. I **don't like** karaoke very much.	
	I **can't stand** karaoke.	**Hate**

A **Write.** Complete the questions about these pastimes. Then write your answers.

Example: Do you like ___computer games___ ?

___No, I don't like computer games very much.___

Level Up!
See page 113.

1. Music

Do you ___like classical music___ ?

_____

3. Sports

Do you _____ ?

_____

2. Shopping

Do you _____ ?

_____

4. Movies

Do you _____ ?

_____

B **Speak.** Ask a partner the questions above. Listen to your partner's answers. Then ask follow-up questions. Use the suggestions below.

For "yes" or "it's OK" answers:	For "no" or "can't stand" answers:
What's your favorite (store)?	Really? Why not?
Who's your favorite (singer)?	

Communicate ▸ Guess My Favorites

A Speak. Make groups and choose a topic. Guess one person's favorite thing. Who guessed correctly? Take turns and keep score.

Example:

A: Guess my favorite color.
B: Blue.
C: I think it's yellow.
A: Yumi is right! My favorite color is yellow.

Happy Birthday To You!

song

season

class

color

magazine

time of day

kind of pet

place at school

Score (1 point for each correct guess)

Your Idea!

B Speak. Who is the best guesser in your group? Tell the class, and then have that student guess the teacher's favorites.

Example: In our group, Yumi is the best guesser.

Useful Expressions
That's interesting.
That's unusual.

Working on Fluency ▶ Comparing Opinions

A 🔘 **4** **Listen.** Ben and Susanna are discussing shopping. Who likes these things? Check [✔] the correct answers.

Ben
- ☐ shopping
- ☐ the mall
- ☐ shopping online

Susanna
- ☐ shopping
- ☐ the mall
- ☐ shopping online

B 🔘 **4** **Write and listen again.** Write *Me too*, *Me neither*, or *Not me* to complete the conversations. Then listen to check your answers.

1. **A:** Do you like shopping?
   B: I love shopping! How about you?
   A: _____. I go shopping almost every day.

2. **A:** I'm crazy about the mall. How about you?
   B: _____. I can't stand the mall.

3. **A:** Really? I can't stand shopping online. How about you?
   B: _____. I use my computer to play games, not shop!

Critical Thinking

Think about polite ways to disagree. Which answer is nicer?

I love the Beatles. How about you? Do you like them?

☐ Well, not really.

☐ No, I don't like them.

C **Write and speak.** Complete the chart. Then tell your classmates and ask their opinions.

Example:
A: I'm crazy about hip-hop. How about you?
B: Me too. I love it.

Three things I'm crazy about:	Three things I can't stand:

Challenge

List your favorite things. Then ask other students whether they like those things too. Find the person with interests most similar to yours.

A **Write.** Fill in the *Things I Love* worksheet on page 23.

B **Speak.** Ask four partners if they like the things in your worksheet. They will answer with the expressions below. Write the points for each partner's answer.

Score

−1	0	+1
I don't like *X*.	*X* is OK.	I like *X*.
I hate *X*.	I'm not sure.	I love *X*.
I can't stand *X*.	I don't know.	I'm crazy about *X*.

Example:

A: Do you like orange juice?
B: Hmm, I don't like it very much.
A: Oh really? What's your favorite morning drink?
B: Coffee.

C **Write and speak.** Add up the total scores for each person. Write their names and scores on the line below. Then tell the class.

_____

-9   **0**   **+9**
very different from me   very similar to me

Example:

Luis is similar to me. We both love coffee, baseball, and classical music.

Presentation Tip

When you say the name of another person, gesture or nod toward that person.

Things I Love

Fill in the charts with your favorites. Then ask your partners (A–D). Write **+1**, **0**, or **–1** for each partner's answers.

Foods

	My answers	Partners' points			
		A	**B**	**C**	**D**
1. My favorite morning drink:	orange juice				
2. A food I love:					
3. Your idea _____ :					

Pastimes

	My answers	Partners' points			
		A	**B**	**C**	**D**
4. A sport I like:					
5. A store I like:					
6. Your idea _____ :					

Movies and Music

	My answers	Partners' points			
		A	**B**	**C**	**D**
7. A TV show I love:					
8. My favorite kind of music:					
9. Your idea _____ :					
	Total Scores				

Do you like orange juice?

Yes, I love it!

Partner A Name: _____

Partner B Name: _____

Partner C Name: _____

Partner D Name: _____

Reflection Time

Write useful words and ideas you learned in this unit.

Design a Town

3

Challenge Preview

Unit Challenge

▸ Design your ideal town.
▸ Explain it to a partner.
▸ Draw your partner's town.

A **Write.** Write three kinds of places you want near your home and three you don't want near your home. Here are some examples:

convenience store

fire station

fast food restaurant

fitness center

train station

I want a . . . near my home.	I don't want a . . . near my home.

B 5 **Write and listen.** Ethan is asking Sang-mi about her ideal town so that he can draw a map of it. Write *in*, *on*, *to*, or *from* to complete the conversation. Then listen to check your answers.

Ethan: Tell me about your ideal town.

Who lives next _____ you?

Sang-mi: My **grandmother**.

Ethan: Does **she** live on the right or _____ the left?

Sang-mi: **She's** on the right.

Ethan: Okay. What are some other places _____ your town?

Sang-mi: Well, there's **a convenience store** across _____ my house.

Ethan: A **convenience store**? That's handy.

C **Speak.** Now practice the conversation with a partner. Then change the words in red to talk about a person you like and a store you like.

Working on Language ▶ Describing Locations

There's	a park **across from** the office building. a farm **in front of** the park. a restaurant **next to** the office building. It's **on the right**.
There are	some mountains **behind** the town.

A Write. Label the items in the picture. Then complete the sentences.

1. There are some trees _____ the **farm**.

2. There's a road _____ the **house**.

3. There's a **lake** _____ the house and apartment building.

4. There's a **river** _____ the farm. It's _____.

5. There's a **restaurant** _____ the office building. It's _____.

B Write and speak. Think of a building near your school. Write three hints about its location. Say the hints. Your partner will guess the place.

1. _____

2. _____

3. _____

Example:

A: It's across from the train station.

B: OK.

A: It's next to Marconi's Pizza.

B: Is it Scoop's Ice Cream?

A: Yes, that's right.

Level Up!
See page 114.

Communicate ▶ Can You Find Me?

A **Speak.** Take turns. Choose one of the windows (1–11) below. A partner will ask questions and then guess which window you are looking out of.

Example:

A: What can you see out of your window?

B: There is a tree in front of me.

A: Is there a field next to the tree?

B: No, there isn't.

A: Is there a farm building near the tree?

B: Yes, there is.

A: You're in window number 1.

B: Yes, that's right.

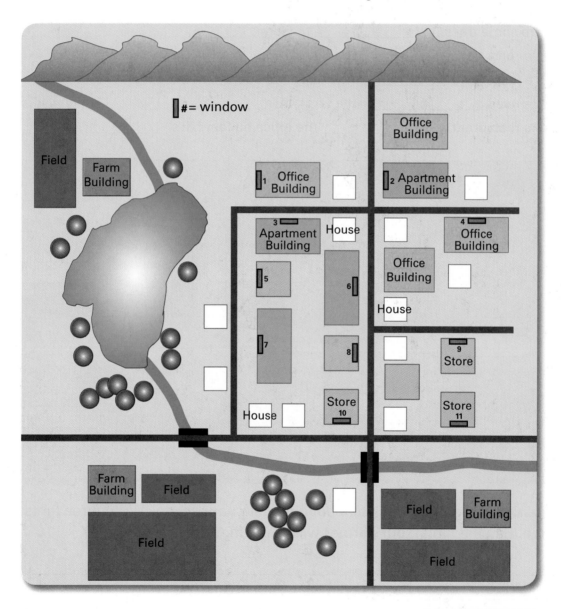

B **Speak.** Draw another window on any building and say what you can see. Can your partner find you?

Example:

There's an office building right in front of me.

Working on Fluency ▶ Confirming Information

A 💿 **6** **Listen.** Yumi is talking to Rey on a cell phone. Check [✔] the place where they are meeting.

☐ pizza place   ☐ movie theater   ☐ game center

B 💿 **6** **Listen again.** Circle the phrases Rey and Yumi use to confirm what each other says.

The movie theater?	Tonight?	Across from the pizza place?
The game center?	The movie?	In ten minutes?

C **Speak.** Tell your partner about the places you like to go in these situations. Your partner will confirm what you say.

▸ when you go shopping
▸ when you go out with your friends
▸ when you go to another city
▸ when you go out to exercise

Example:
A: There are some stores near my house.
B: Some stores?
A: Yeah, there's a convenience store and a clothing store . . .

Critical Thinking

Think about why you might repeat what someone says. Read these reasons and add one more:
– What you hear makes you angry.
– You are not sure you heard something correctly.
– _____
  _____

Challenge

Design your ideal town. Then tell your partner about it.

A **Write.** Decide what shops, companies, natural scenery (mountains, the ocean, etc.), and whose houses to put near your house. Label the buildings. Then add six more places.

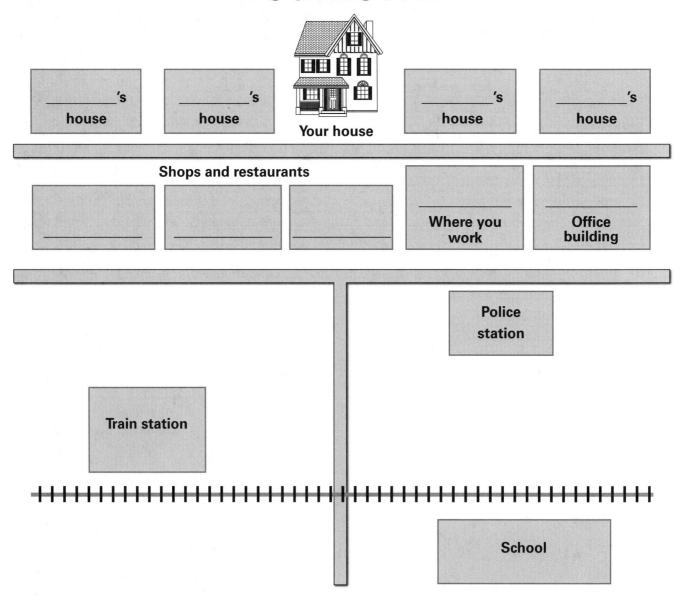

Your Town

_____'s house

_____'s house

Your house

_____'s house

_____'s house

Shops and restaurants

Where you work

Office building

Police station

Train station

School

B Speak and write. Your partner will tell you about his or her ideal town. (Don't look at your partner's book.) Ask questions and complete the map below.

Example:

A: Next to my house on the right is my teammate Sam's house.

B: Why your teammate?

A: So that we can go to the fitness center together.

Your Town

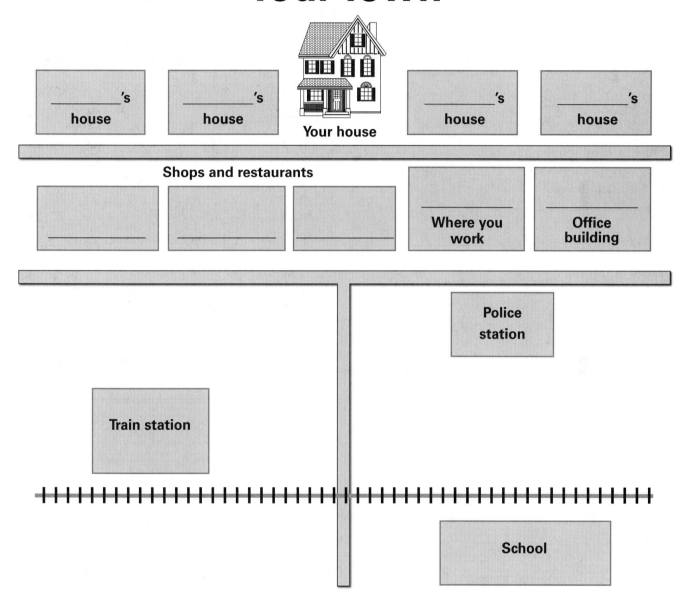

C Speak. Tell the class some interesting things about your partner's town.

Example: Kirsten has a theme park near her house. I think that's great!

Reflection Time

Write useful words and ideas you learned in this unit.

Neighborhood Walking Tour

Think of places in your neighborhood that you like. Make a walking tour past those places and tell your classmates about them.

A Read. A student is telling his classmates about his neighborhood walking tour. Do you have any places like these in your neighborhood?

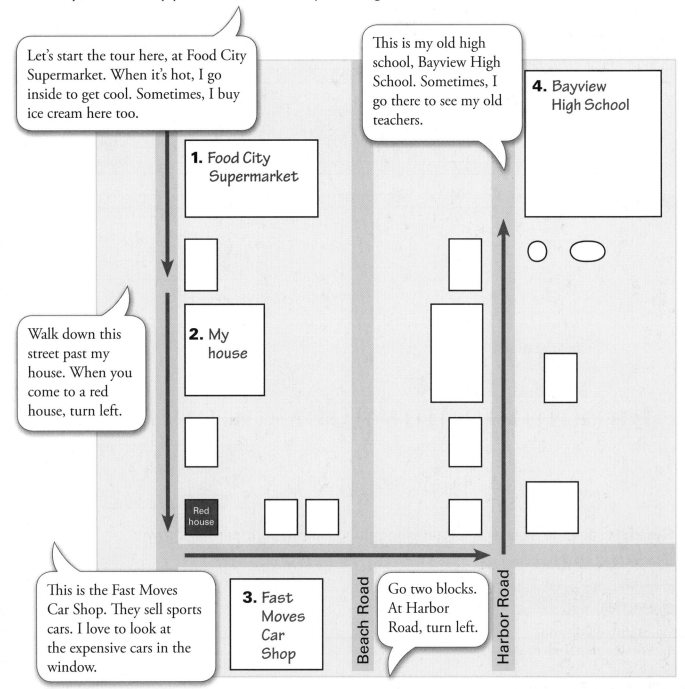

Let's start the tour here, at Food City Supermarket. When it's hot, I go inside to get cool. Sometimes, I buy ice cream here too.

This is my old high school, Bayview High School. Sometimes, I go there to see my old teachers.

4. Bayview High School

1. Food City Supermarket

Walk down this street past my house. When you come to a red house, turn left.

2. My house

Red house

This is the Fast Moves Car Shop. They sell sports cars. I love to look at the expensive cars in the window.

3. Fast Moves Car Shop

Beach Road

Go two blocks. At Harbor Road, turn left.

Harbor Road

B Write. Think of some interesting places in your town, such as the ones below. Write notes about them.

a supermarket	a place with a nice view	a vending machine
an interesting old tree	an interesting building	a place you go with friends
a relative's house	a place where you can sit and rest	

Place	Notes
Food City Supermarket	When it's hot, I go inside to get cool. Sometimes, I buy ice cream too.

C Draw. Make a map of your walking tour on a sheet of paper. Write in street names, building names, and your interesting places.

D Speak. Show other students your map, give directions for your walking tour, and tell them about your interesting places. They will ask questions.

Useful Words for Directions

Start here at (place).	Go to (place).	At (place/street), turn (right/left).
Walk down this street.	Go past (place).	When you come to (place), turn (right/left).

Example:

A: When you come to a school, turn right. There are some seats next to it. Sometimes, I sit there.

B: Why there?

A: It's quiet and peaceful. I go there to relax.

What's for Dinner? 4

Challenge Preview

Unit Challenge

▶ Do an information gap activity.
▶ Find out what someone is making for dinner.

A **Write.** Mark the dishes with ✔ (like), ✘ (don't like), or **?** (have never tried).

☐ Mexican tacos

☐ Turkish shish kabob

☐ Korean kimchee

☐ Japanese sushi

☐ Thai fried noodles

☐ American pumpkin pie

☐ Italian pizza

B 🔘 **7** **Write and listen.** Yumi and James are looking at two different pictures of a kitchen. They are trying to find out what foods a friend used to make dinner. Complete the conversation with *in*, *on*, or *at*. Then listen to check your answers.

James: Look _____ the kitchen counter _____ the left.

Yumi: _____ the left?

James: Yes, that's right. How many **onions** are there?

Yumi: _____ my picture, there are **three onions**.

James: There's only **one onion** _____ my picture.

Yumi: So, he used **two** of the **onions**!

C **Speak.** Now practice the conversation with a partner. Then change the words in red to talk about these pictures.

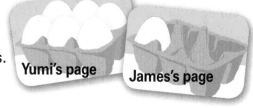

Yumi's page   James's page

Working on Language ▶ Talking about Food

Questions	Answers
Is there **any** garlic?	Yes, there**'s some** garlic.
Are there **any** cherries?	No, there **aren't**.
Is there **any** orange juice?	Yes, there **are two** bottles of orange juice.
How many carrots **are** there?	There **are three** carrots.

A **Write.** Label as many foods as you can. Then complete the conversations.

A: Are there any onions?

B: _____

A: Is there any rice?

B: _____

A: How many peaches are there?

B: _____

A: Are there any oranges?

B: _____

A: Is there _____?

B: Yes, there is one loaf of bread.

A: _____?

B: No, there isn't any fish.

A: _____

B: Yes, there are two bags of spaghetti.

A: _____

B: Yes, there's one bottle of cooking oil.

B **Write and speak.** What do you use to make these dishes? Fill in the chart and then compare with a partner.

Pizza	Fruit Salad	Sandwich

Communicate ▶ Mystery Dish Quiz

A Write. Think of two dishes you know how to make. What ingredients do you need?

Mystery Dish 1

Mystery Dish 2

B Speak and write. A partner will tell you the ingredients in one of the mystery dishes. Write them down. Then ask *yes/no* questions to find out what the mystery dish is.

Example:

A: There are some eggs, butter, and cheese in my mystery dish. There's some milk in it, too.

B: Is it a breakfast dish?

A: Yes.

B: Hmm. I don't know. What is it?

A: My mystery dish is a cheese omelet.

Mystery Dish

eggs

butter

cheese

milk

Useful **Expressions**

It's a snack.

It's a breakfast/lunch/ dinner dish.

It's a dessert.

Level Up!
See page 115.

Working on Fluency ▶ Interrupting

A 🔘 **8** **Listen.** Adam and Lauren are talking on their cell phones. Write the name of each person under the place where he or she is.

1. _____

2. _____

3. _____

B 🔘 **8** **Listen again.** Write in the missing words or phrases.

> Wait.   Hang on.   Excuse me?   Sorry.

1. Lauren: We need two cartons of eggs.

   Adam: _____ Two cartons of eggs?

2. Lauren: Buy four bags of flour.

   Adam: _____ Four?

3. Lauren: Buy three packs of butter.

   Adam: _____ Why so many?

> ### 💡 Critical Thinking
>
> Think about when you might need to interrupt to get the details right. Check [✔] the more likely situation.
>
> ☐ Listening to a friend talking about a trip she took.
>
> ☐ Getting driving directions.

C **Write and speak.** Make a shopping list for a class party. Then tell a partner. Your partner will interrupt, check what you say, and write it down.

Example:

A: On my shopping list, I have eight boxes of cookies and . . .

B: Wait. Eight boxes of cookies?

Your shopping list:

_____ box(es) of cookies

_____ bag(s) of potato chips

_____ bottle(s) of iced tea

_____ _____ of _____

_____ _____ of _____

Your partner's shopping list:

_____ box(es) of cookies

_____ bag(s) of potato chips

_____ bottle(s) of iced tea

_____ _____ of _____

_____ _____ of _____

Challenge: Information Gap

> Your neighbor Freddy cooked dinner tonight. Compare pictures A and B of Freddy's kitchen with a partner. What did he make for dinner?

A **Do the information gap activity.** Follow these instructions.

1 Get into pairs: Student A and Student B.

2 Sit so that you cannot see your partner's book.

> In my picture, there are three onions. How many are there in your picture?

3 **Student A:** Look at page 37. **Student B:** Look at page 94. Do NOT look at your partner's page.

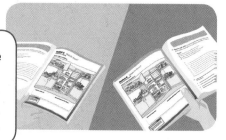

4 Compare what's in the kitchen before and after Freddy cooked dinner. What did he use? What did he make for dinner?

5 Quietly show your answers to the teacher.

B **Speak.** When you finish, plan a dinner party with your partner. Discuss what dishes to make and what groceries to buy.

Example:
A: Let's make a chocolate cake for our party, OK?
B: All right. What do we need to buy?

What's for dinner? Before Freddy Cooked Dinner

What did Freddy use?

1. _____   5. _____
2. _____   6. _____
3. _____   7. _____
4. _____   8. _____

What did Freddy make for dinner?

Reflection Time

Write useful words and ideas you learned in this unit.

Challenge Preview

Unit Challenge

▸ Make a new holiday and describe it to your classmates.
▸ Make a poster and vote on the best ideas.

A Check [✔]. Which of these real holidays do you want to celebrate?

☐ **Festival of Sleep Day**—sleep late or take nap.

☐ **National Hugging Day**—hug family and friends.

☐ **Backward Day**—read, write, and wear clothes backwards.

☐ **Dress Up Your Pet Day**—your pet wears fun clothing.

B 🔘 **9 Write and listen.** Kirsten is telling James about a holiday she made. Write *at* or *on* to complete the conversation. Then listen to check your answers.

Kirsten: My holiday is **Pajama Day**. It's _____ May 9.

James: I see. So how do you celebrate it?

Kirsten: _____ this day, we **wear our pajamas everywhere**.

James: Uh, really? Do you **wear your pajamas to school**?

Kirsten: Yes. **At home, at school, everywhere!**

James: Oh, I see. Anything else?

Kirsten: Uh-huh. _____ midnight, we **have a pajama party**!

C Speak. Now practice the conversation with a partner. Then change the words in red to talk about this new holiday.

▸ No Meat Day
▸ October 16
▸ don't eat any meat
▸ only eat vegetables and fruit
▸ It's very healthy
▸ go out for cheeseburgers

Working on Language ▶ Explaining Holiday Routines

> My family has a special dinner on my **father's birthday**.
>
> We **never** go out to eat.   **0%**
> We **sometimes** invite friends over.
> We **usually** make his favorite food.
> We **always** play games after dinner.   **100%**

A **Write.** Fill in the blanks with *never*, *sometimes*, *usually*, or *always* to make these sentences true for you. Then write two sentences of your own.

1. I _____ have a party on my birthday.

2. I _____ spend my birthday with my family.

3. I _____ go to a restaurant on my birthday.

4. I _____ get birthday cards on my birthday.

5. _____
   _____

6. _____
   _____

B **Write and speak.** Think of two other things you do on your birthday. Write them. Then compare with a partner.

Level Up!
See page 116.

1. _____.

2. _____.

Communicate ▶ Special Days

A **Speak and write.** Work with other students. Make a list of at least six special days you celebrate.

> **I** _usually_ **do something special on** _the last day of school_.
> (how often)   (day)

or

> **I** _always_ **celebrate** _Valentine's Day_.
> (how often)   (day)

Special Days List

• **the last day of school**   • **Valentine's Day**

B **Speak.** Ask what your partner does on each of the special days. There are some ideas below to help.

Useful Expressions

That sounds fun.
That's interesting.

Example:

A: What do you usually do on the last day of school?
B: I usually go out with my friends.
A: Where do you go?
B: Sometimes we go to a restaurant, and sometimes we just go shopping.

visit relatives

eat special food

decorate the house

don't do anything special

send greeting cards

watch a special program on TV

visit a temple

say a holiday greeting

watch fireworks

A 🔟 **Listen.** A Thai student is talking about her favorite holiday, Songkran. Check [✔] the ways she celebrates.

☐ She goes back to her hometown.

☐ She watches fireworks.

☐ She goes out to eat.

☐ She throws water.

B 🔟 **Listen again.** Circle the four pause fillers the speakers use.

Well	You know	Um/uh
Hmm	Maybe	Let's see

C Write and speak. Answer the questions. Discuss these topics with your partner. Use pause fillers as you speak.

▸ What is your favorite holiday? _____

▸ What holiday is the most expensive for you? _____

▸ What do you want for your birthday? _____

Example:
A: What is your favorite holiday?
B: Well, let's see, it's, um, "Kodomo no Hi."
A: Oh, "Children's Day." Why?

💡 **Critical Thinking**

Think of pause fillers in your own language that are used like these:
1. *Um* (when getting the next words ready)
2. *Let's see* (when figuring something out)
3. *Maybe* (when you aren't sure)

Challenge

Make a new holiday and tell your classmates about it. Vote on the best ideas.

A **Speak and write.** As a class, brainstorm ideas for new holidays. Write down any interesting ideas you hear.

No Cell Phone Day

Red Shoes Day

Use Your Cell Phone Anytime Day

Shopaholic Day

How about a No Cell Phone Day? On this day, we can't use our cell phones.

OK, or how about Use Your Cell Phone Anytime Day?

B **Write and draw.** Think of an interesting holiday idea and make a poster for it on a piece of paper. Include the following:

▶ the name of the holiday
▶ the date
▶ a picture or symbol for this holiday
▶ three or more things you do on this day

No Meat
October 16

• We don't eat any meat all day.
• We only eat vegetables and fruit.
• At midnight, we go out for cheeseburgers.

C **Speak and write.** Ask other students about their holidays. Ask questions and take notes in the chart below.

▶ What's your new holiday?
▶ When is it?
▶ What do you do on that day?

Name of Holiday	When	What People Do on This Day
No Meat Day	Oct 16	don't eat any meat

D **Vote.** Choose the best holidays and give awards like these. Which holiday would you most like to celebrate?

The most fun is

_____.

The most useful is

_____.

The most unusual is

_____.

Reflection Time

Write useful words and ideas you learned in this unit.

The Everyday Hero Award

Challenge Preview

Unit Challenge

▸ Make an award for someone who is nice to you.
▸ Tell other students about it.

A **Check [✔].** Which of these people do you see at or near your school? Do you know any of their names?

☐ cleaning person

☐ bus driver

☐ receptionist

☐ cook

B 🔘 11 **Write and listen.** Sang-mi is telling Rey about her award. Write *she* or *her* to complete the conversation. Then listen to check your answers.

Sang-mi:	My award is for the **receptionist**.
Rey:	The **receptionist**? Does _____ work in the **main office**?
Sang-mi:	Yes. _____ works in the **main office**, but I don't know _____ name.
Rey:	So, why _____?
Sang-mi:	Well, _____ always **smiles and says "hello."**
Rey:	Really? _____ sounds friendly.

C **Speak.** Now practice the conversation with a partner. Then change the words in red to talk about Rey's award.

▸ cook
▸ cafeteria
▸ remembers my name

Working on Language ▸ Talking About People You Know

Level Up!
See page 117.

Question	Answer
Do you know Mr. Lin?	Yes, I **do**. / No, I **don't**.
Is he the school guard?	Yes, he **is**. / No, he **isn't**.
Does he work at the front gate?	Yes, he **does**. / No, he **doesn't**.

A Circle. Complete the conversations with the correct form of *do* or *be*.

1. **A:** (Does / Is) Sarah work in the cafeteria?

   B: Yes, she (is / does).

2. **A:** (Is / Does) she the math teacher?

   B: No, she (isn't / doesn't). She's the new English teacher.

3. **A:** (Do / Are) you know Ms. Esaki?

   B: (Is / Does) she the school nurse?

   A: Yes, that's right. She's really nice.

4. **A:** (Are / Do) you know the tennis coach?

   B: I think so. (Does / Is) he wear glasses?

   A: No, he (isn't / doesn't).

B Write and speak. Write three hints about a person who works at your school and who everyone knows. Then tell your hints to your partner. Your partner will guess who it is.

> Is it the Spanish teacher?

> Yes, that's right!

Example:

This person is a teacher.

She does not teach our class.

She has an office in this building.

Your turn:

1. _____

2. _____

3. _____

Communicate ▶ Who Helps You the Most?

A **Write.** Who does these things for you? Write their names in the boxes.

Example: My father takes me to the movies.

Who helps you with your homework? _____

Who does fun things with you? _____

Who makes you laugh? _____

Who makes you happy? _____

That one.

Who gives you advice? _____

Who listens to your problems? _____

Who gives you things? _____

Your Idea!

_____
_____

B **Speak.** Your partner will ask you these and other questions. Answer with specific examples of how the people above help you.

Example:

A: Who does fun things with you?

B: My father takes me to the movies. He's really nice.

A 🔘 **12** **Listen.** Peggy is talking about her boss. Check [✔] the things her boss does for her.

☐ He takes her to movies.

☐ He buys her presents.

☐ He takes her to restaurants.

☐ He takes her shopping.

B 🔘 **12** **Listen again.** How does the man respond to Peggy? Circle the responses you hear.

1. He sounds nice. / He sounds friendly.

2. That sounds interesting. / That sounds fun.

3. That sounds strange. / That sounds terrible.

C **Write and speak.** Complete the sentences. Then read them to your partner. Your partner will respond with phrases like those above.

1. Let's go to _____ together.
      (where?)

2. I want to give _____ to _____.
      (what?)   (whom?)

3. _____ is sick today.
      (who?)

4. _____.
      (your idea)

Example:

A: Let's go to a movie together.

B: Oh, that sounds fun. What movie?

💡 Critical Thinking

Think about what kind of information these verbs are used for. Read the sentence and match the verbs and information.

Ellen _____ happy.
   a. looks
   b. sounds
   c. seems
___ She says she feels great.
___ She is smiling.
___ She does happy things in general.

Challenge

Think of someone who helps you, does nice things, or works hard. Create an Everyday Hero Award and show it to the other students.

A **Write.** Look at the example chart. Fill in the chart below and the award on the next page.

Example:

What's the person's name?	I don't know his name.
What's the person's job? Where does he or she work?	The school guard. The front gate.
Why does this person get the award? Check [✔] boxes and give some examples.	☑ Friendly ☐ Kind ☐ Hardworking ☐ Cheerful ☑ Helpful ☐ _____ He always says "good morning" to everyone. He helps me with my bicycle.

What's the person's name?	
What's the person's job? Where does he or she work?	
Why does this person get the award? Check [✔] boxes and give some examples.	☐ Friendly ☐ Kind ☐ Hardworking ☐ Cheerful ☐ Helpful ☐ _____

B **Speak.** Ask other students about their awards. Find out whom the award is for and what's special about that person.

Example:

A: Who's your award for?
B: My award is for the school guard.
A: Does he work at the front gate?
B: Yes, but I don't know his name. He's about 50 . . .

Everyday Hero Award
Awarded to: The school guard
Because: He is friendly. He always says "good morning" to everyone.
He is helpful. I ride my bicycle to school. There are many bicycles in the bicycle parking lot, so it is hard to get my bicycle out. Sometimes he helps me.
HERO
Signed:

Everyday Hero Award

Awarded to: _____

Because: _____

_____

_____

_____

_____

_____

HERO

Signed: _____

Presentation Tip

Bring the listeners into your topic by asking them questions. For example, you can ask: "Do you know him? Has he ever helped you?"

Reflection Time

Write useful words and ideas you learned in this unit.

Who's Who Around School

Make a Who's Who page about someone interesting at (or around) your school. Then tell your classmates.

A **Read.** A student is talking about a person she interviewed. What questions did she ask him?

> This is Mr. Liu. He teaches Chinese.

> His dream is to write a book about birds.

> He has 6 birds in cages in his living room. They are really noisy, but he likes their songs.

Who's Who at Excel College

Mr. Jiang Liu

Name: Jiang Liu

Job: Chinese language teacher

Hometown: Shanghai, China

Hobbies: singing, bird watching, tennis

Dream: He wants to write a book.

Something interesting about him:

- He has six birds.
- He speaks four languages.

Message to us: Study Chinese too! It's an interesting language.

B **Write.** As a class, decide on someone for each student to interview. Then, write your person's name below.

a teacher

a cleaning person

a shop owner

a police officer

I will interview _____.

C **Prepare.** As a class, decide what information to put on your Who's Who pages. Here are some ideas.

name	photo/drawing	job
family	hometown	living where now
hobbies or interests	a favorite CD/food/color	dream
an interesting fact	a message to our class	why I like this person

D **Interview.** Interview the person and fill in your worksheet.

Interview topics	
Name	
Job	

E **Speak.** Present your worksheet to your classmates. When you finish, you can put your worksheet pages together to make a class Who's Who book.

Example:

This is Mr. Liu. He's a Chinese teacher at our school. He's from Shanghai, China.

Now Hiring

Challenge Preview

Unit Challenge

▸ Design an original job.
▸ Tell other students about it.

A **Number.** Which of these part-time jobs do you want to do? Rank them from 1 to 4.

☐ zoo employee

☐ store clerk

☐ game tester

☐ gardener

B 🔘 13 **Write and listen.** Ethan is telling Kirsten about a job. Write *a* or *the* to complete the conversation. Then listen to check your answers.

Kirsten: What is the job?

Ethan: Zoo employee.

Kirsten: What do I have to do?

Ethan: Well, first, you have to **wash** _____ **elephants.** Then you have to **feed** _____ **lions.**

Kirsten: You're kidding! It sounds like _____ really **dangerous** job.

Ethan: You're right. It is.

Zoo Employee

C **Speak.** Now practice the conversation with a partner. Then change the words in red to talk about working as a gardener.

▸ gardener
▸ cut the grass
▸ water the plants
▸ easy job

Questions	Answers
What **do I have to do**?	You **have to drive** a taxi from nine until five.
Do I have to have a driver's license?	**Yes**, you **do**.
Do I have to wear a uniform?	**No**, you **don't**.

A **Write.** What do these employees have to do in these jobs? Write two things for each job using the ideas below.

tell children stories	put things in shopping bags	give children snacks
serve food	clean tables	say, "Thanks for shopping here."

Babysitter

Example: Babysitters have to play with children.

1. _____

2. _____

Your Idea: _____

Store clerk

1. _____

2. _____

Your Idea: _____

Level Up!
See page 118.

Server

1. _____

2. _____

Your Idea: _____

B **Write and speak.**
Add one more thing each employee has to do for the job. Then compare your ideas with other students.

A babysitter has to put children to bed.

They sometimes have to clean, too.

Useful Verbs

handle
take care of
use
work

Communicate ▶ Mystery Job Game

A **Read.** Yumi and Ethan are trying to guess which of the pictures below is Rey's mystery job. Read the conversation and write the answer.

Example:

Rey: What's my mystery job?

Yumi: Do you have to sell things?

Rey: Yes.

Ethan: Let's see. Do you have to put clothes on shelves?

Rey: Sometimes.

Yumi: Are you a _____?
(job)

Rey: Yes! That's right.

clothes shop employee

mail carrier

drugstore clerk

English teacher

home care giver

construction worker

restaurant cook

flight attendant

supermarket clerk

security guard

tour guide

B **Speak.** Make groups. One member chooses a job. The other members take turns asking yes/no questions to guess the job.

Do you have to _____?

Are you a _____? (You can only ask this question once.)

Useful Expressions

No, not really.
Sometimes.
I'm not sure.

A 🔘 **14** **Listen.** A man is talking about his new job. Check [✔] the two things that he has to do.

B 🔘 **14** **Listen again.** The listener uses certain phrases to show surprise four times. Number the phrases from 1 to 4 in the order you hear them.

a. ___ You're kidding!

b. ___ A what?

c. ___ No. Really?

d. ___ I can't believe it!

C **Write and speak.** Write four sentences like the model below about one of these unusual jobs. Tell a partner. Your partner will respond with the expressions above.

▸ fashion designer
▸ dog trainer
▸ theme-park employee
▸ stunt person

1. I have a new job. I'm a _____fashion designer_____.

2. I have to ___go to Paris every week___ .

3. I make _____$500_____ an hour.

4. Sometimes, they ___give me free clothes___ .

Example:

A: I have a new job. I'm a fashion designer.

B: A what?

A: I'm a fashion designer. I have to go to Paris every week.

B: No. Really?

A: Yes, it's true. I make $500 an hour.

B: You're kidding!

> 💡 **Critical Thinking**
>
> Think about how hearing information you do not expect is surprising. Check [✔] the most surprising sentences and write one more.
>
> ☐ At my part-time job, I make $80 an hour.
> ☐ The child I babysit is 3 years old.
> ☐ I like apples on my pizza.
>
> **Your Idea:**
> _____
> _____

Challenge

Think of an interesting job. Write a job description and then explain the job to your classmates.

A **Discuss.** Which job would you like to have? Check [✔] one and compare your answers with a partner.

☐ **Car Shop Assistant**
You help car mechanics fix cars.

☐ **Movie Extra**
You play a gladiator in a movie.

☐ **Children's English Teacher**
You teach English to young children.

B **Draw and write.** Draw a simple picture and write a job description like this. Use the front and back of a piece of paper.

Front of paper:

A simple picture of the job:

What's the name of the job?   Zoo employee

What are the hours?   Monday through Friday, 10 to 7

What does it pay? $10 an hour

Back of paper:

What *do you have to do?*
- You have to take care of animals in a zoo.
- You have to feed the lions, elephants, and monkeys in the morning. Be careful!
- You have to wash the animals in the afternoon. The monkeys don't like it.
- You have to clean cages. Cleaning the elephant cage is the hardest.

What kind of person do you have to be?
- You have to like animals.
- You have to be strong.

Interesting points:
- You can get free passes to the zoo.
- You can take a one-month vacation in the winter.

C Speak and write. Talk to three students about their interesting jobs. Ask the questions in activity B. Then ask follow-up questions. Take notes on what you hear.

Job 1	
Job 2	
Job 3	

D Write. Choose one job you want and fill in the chart.

Job	Interesting points

Reflection Time

Write useful words and ideas you learned in this unit.

Family Ties

Challenge Preview

Unit Challenge

▸ Do an information gap activity.
▸ Find out who the people in the photos are.

A **Check [✓].** Which statements are true for your family?

☐ One of my relatives is a baby.

☐ Some of my ancestors came from another country.

☐ One of my relatives is a farmer.

☐ My family has a picture of a great-grandfather or great-grandmother.

B 🔘 **15** **Write and listen.** Rey and Sang-mi are talking about John's family photos. They are trying to find out who the people are. Write *his*, *they*, and *you* to complete the conversation. Then listen to check your answers.

Sang-mi:	I have some old pictures of John's family. Is one of _____ relatives a **police officer**?
Rey:	Yes. _____ name is **Billy**.
Sang-mi:	How do _____ spell that?
Rey:	**B-I-L-L-Y**. Did _____ get that?
Sang-mi:	Yes, thanks. Um. How are _____ related?
Rey:	**He's _____ grandfather**.
Sang-mi:	So, **he's his grandfather**. I see.

C **Speak.** Now practice the conversation with a partner. Then change the words in red to talk about the teacher in this photo.

Aunt Yuki and her students

Working on Language ▶ Talking about Family

Asking about a photo	Answer	More Information
Who's this?	She's one of my relatives.	Her name is Ann Smith.
How are you related?	She's my aunt.	She's married with two children.
Who's this?	He was one of my ancestors.	His name was John.
How are you related?	He was my great-grandfather.	He was born in 1910, and he died in 1978.

A Match and label. Connect the sentences and then fill in the chart with the underlined relationship words.

Level Up! See page 119.

1. My <u>wife</u> and I have two children. •
2. My <u>aunt</u> and <u>uncle</u> have a son. •
3. My <u>mother</u> and <u>father</u> have two children. •
4. My <u>brother</u> is married to my <u>sister-in-law</u>. •
5. My <u>grandfather</u> and <u>grandmother</u> have two children.
6. My <u>great-grandfather</u>, Ben, was a farmer. •

• One of them is me!
• He's John, my <u>cousin</u>.
• We have a <u>son</u> and a <u>daughter</u>.
• They're my <u>mother</u> and my uncle.
• He was born in 1910, and he died in 1981.

• Their children are my <u>nephew</u> and <u>niece</u>.

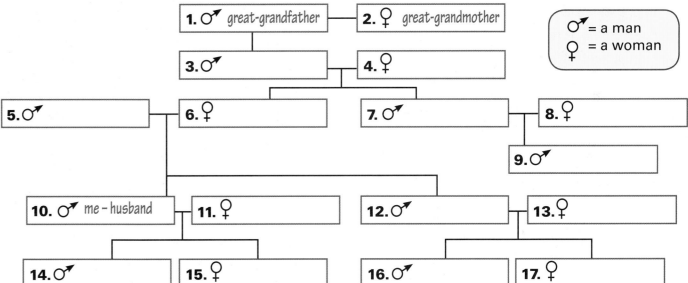

B Write and speak. Make two quiz questions like the example. Then quiz a partner.

Example:

Question: Who's the father of the father of my father?   (My great-grandfather)

1. Question: _____

2. Question: _____

Communicate ▶ Who's This?

A Write. Draw two family members or relatives in the photo frames and write their names.

_____
(name)

_____
(name)

B Speak and write. Look at your partner's pictures. Ask questions about each person and fill in the chart.

Useful Expressions

I'm not sure.
I don't know.

Q: Who's this?　　　　　　**A:** Her name is Ann Smith.
Q: How are you related?　　**A:** She's my aunt.
Q: How old is she?　　　　 **A:** I'm not sure, maybe about 50.
Q: Is she married?　　　　　**A:** Yes. Her husband's name is Juan.
Q: Does she have any children?　**A:** Yes, two daughters.
Q: Does she have a job?　　 **A:** Yes, she does. She's a shop assistant.

	Person 1	Person 2
Name		
Relationship		
Age		
Married		
Children		
Job		
_____ (Your own question)		

Working on Fluency ▶ Clarifying

A 🔘 **16** **Listen.** A lawyer is telling a woman some news about her great-grandfather. What did the great-grandfather give the woman? Check [✔] the correct picture.

B 🔘 **16** **Listen again.** Circle the phrases the woman uses to check what the lawyer is saying.

Please say that again.	Once again, please.
How do you spell that?	Sorry. I don't understand.
What was that?	Did you say . . . ?

Critical Thinking

Think about when you need to use clarifying expressions. Here are some ideas:
- having a discussion in a noisy place
- writing down what someone says

Your idea: _____
_____

C **Write and speak.** Fill in your information in the chart. Then fill in your partner's information by asking questions and using the phrases above to check.

Example:
A: What's your email address?
B: It's mimi.forever@gmail.com.
A: Um . . . How do you spell that?
B: It's M-I-M . . .

	Your answers	Your partner's answers
Email address		
Phone number		
Mother's first name		
A foreign product you use		

Challenge: Information Gap

Student A: Use this page. **Student B**: Go to page 92.

Talk about Betty's family to find out who the people in her family photos are.
Then talk about John's family too.

A **Do the information gap activity.** (See Unit 4 page 36 for more information.)
This is Betty's family tree. First complete the relationship words. Then your partner (Student
B) will ask questions about Betty's family.

Example:

Student B: Who's Julie?   **Student A:** She's Betty's grandmother.
Student B: What's her husband's name?   **Student A:** William.
Student B: How do you spell that?   **Student A:** W-I-L-L-I-A-M.

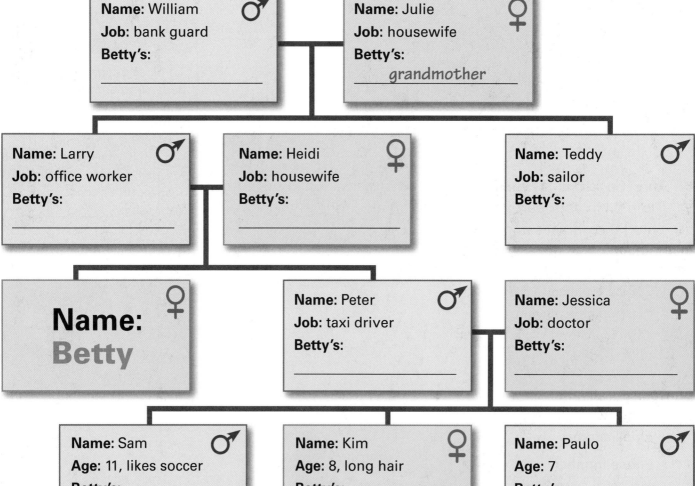

B **Speak.** These are pictures of John's family members. Ask questions to find out the people's names and their relationships to John.

Example:

Student A: Does John have a relative who's a police officer?

Student A: How are they related?

Student B: Yes. His name is Billy.

Student B: He's John's grandfather.

♂ **Name:** Billy

John's: _____

Job: _____

♀ **Name:** _____

John's: _____

Job: _____

Children's Names:

1. _____

2. _____

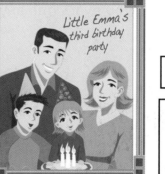

Little Emma's third birthday party

♂ **John**

♀ **Name:** _____

John's: _____

Job: _____

♂ **Name:** _____

John's: _____

Age: _____

♀ **Name:** _____

John's: _____

Age: _____

♂ **Name:** _____

John's: _____

Job: _____

♀ **Name:** _____

John's: _____

Job: _____

Child's Name:

_____

Winners 1982 Dance contest

♀ **Name:** _____

John's: _____

Job: _____

♂ **Name:** _____

John's: _____

Job: _____

Age: _____

C **Speak.** John and Betty have one mysterious relative who is the same person! Can you find that person? If so, try to figure out what happened in his or her life.

Reflection Time

Write useful words and ideas you learned in this unit.

Timeline

Challenge Preview

Unit Challenge

▸ Make a timeline of important events in your life.
▸ Ask other students about events in their lives.

A Check [✓]. Have you ever done any of these things?

☐ got an award

☐ had an accident

☐ traveled abroad

☐ performed on stage

B 🔘 **17 Write and listen.** James is telling Yumi about an accident he had. Write the words below to complete the conversation. Then listen to check your answers.

> suddenly   still   really

Yumi: What's this?

James: When I was a **high school** student, I was on the **soccer** team. I _____ loved it.

Yumi: The **soccer** team? Wow! That's cool.

James: Yeah, it was. But in one game, I _____ got hit in the **face** with the ball.

Yumi: Oh, that's terrible. Were you hurt?

James: Yes, a little bit, but we _____ won!

C Speak. Now practice the conversation with a partner. Then change the words in red to talk about James's experience playing tennis.

▸ college
▸ tennis
▸ head

Working on Language ▶ Talking About Past Events

When	What happened
When I was a child,	I **went** to Spain.
A few years **ago**,	I **bought** a guitar.
In 2005,	I **had** a car accident.
Recently,	I **joined** a music club.

A **Write.** Make sentences about these events using simple past tense verbs.

▶ belong to a club   ▶ put on a play

Example: In <u>high school</u>,

I <u>belonged to the drama club</u> and we
<u>put on a play</u>.

▶ go shopping   ▶ get lost

1. When I was a _____,

I _____ and I

_____.

▶ get a new job   ▶ move to Paris

2. In _____,

my father _____ and my family

_____.

▶ write a school newspaper article   ▶ win a prize

3. _____

_____.

B **Write and speak.** Think of your own experiences on these or other topics. Write about two experiences and then tell a partner.

Example: <u>When I was 16, I went to Europe. It was very exciting!</u>

a trip   a job   a concert   a sports event

Level Up!
See page 120.

1. _____

2. _____

Communicate ▶ My Interesting Life

A **Write.** Imagine you are 80 years old. You are remembering the important things that happened in your life. Fill in your memories with made-up information.

In 2020, I became a kangaroo farmer.

Life Story Survey

What was your job?
- ☐ rock musician
- ☐ company president
- ☐ professional athlete
- ☐ Your idea: _____

In _____, I became a(n) _____.

Did you travel?
- ☐ Mount Everest
- ☐ Paris
- ☐ Hollywood
- ☐ Your idea: _____

Yes, when I was _____, I went to _____.

Did you get married?
- ☐ a movie star
- ☐ a famous chef
- ☐ a classmate
- ☐ Your idea: _____

Yes, in_____, I married _____.

What else did you do? Your idea: When _____,
I _____.
In _____,
I _____.

B **Speak.** Ask about your partner's life. Ask follow-up questions too.

Example:
A: What was your job?
B: I was a professional athlete.
A: That's interesting. What sport?
B: Beach volleyball.

Useful Expressions
That's nice.
That's too bad.
Really? Why?

Working on Fluency ▶ Showing Interest or Concern

A 🔘 **18** **Listen.** A student is telling his friend a story. What follow-up question do you think she asks about each situation? Match the questions to the pictures. Then listen to check.

☐ **1.** Was it **fun?**   ☐ **2.** Was the driver **angry?**   ☐ **3.** Were you **scared?**   ☐ **4.** Was anyone **hurt?**

B **Write.** Use the adjectives above and below (in blue) to write a follow-up question for each sentence.

sad   surprised   proud   worried   embarrassed

1. I waited for my sister for two hours.   Were you _____?
2. Yuko caught a cold and couldn't go to the party.   Was she _____?
3. A bird landed on my sister's head.   _____?
4. Andy spilled milk all over his pants.   _____?

C **Speak.** Tell a partner about an embarrassing experience. Your partner will ask questions like those above.

Example:
A: A few days ago, I went to the wrong classroom.
B: Was the teacher surprised?

💡 **Critical Thinking**

Think about other reasons people ask follow-up questions like these. Check two reasons:

☐ to show the story is interesting

☐ to show they are listening

☐ to show they want to change the topic

Challenge

Create a timeline of the major events in your life. Then share your personal stories with your classmates.

A Write. Think of four important events in your life. Fill in the chart. Then draw pictures (just pictures, not words) on the timeline on the next page.

Example:

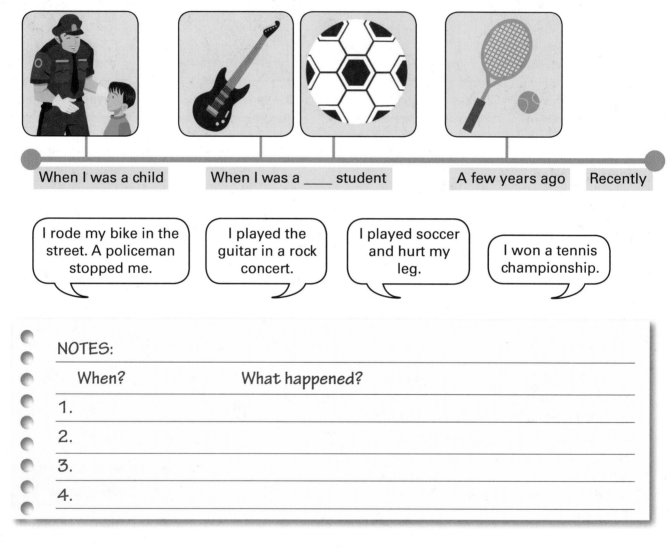

When I was a child

When I was a ____ student

A few years ago   Recently

I rode my bike in the street. A policeman stopped me.

I played the guitar in a rock concert.

I played soccer and hurt my leg.

I won a tennis championship.

NOTES:

When?	What happened?
1.	
2.	
3.	
4.	

B Speak. Show your timeline to a partner. Your partner will ask you questions about it.

Example:

A: What's this?

B: Recently, my family went to Europe. We went to Italy, Greece, and Turkey.

A: That's great. Were you excited?

B: Yes, of course.

My Life Timeline

When I was a child   When I was a ____ student   A few years ago   Recently

Presentation Tip

Speak in short phrases instead of long sentences. "One day . . . when I was a student . . . a teacher . . . came to my house."

Reflection Time

Write useful words and ideas you learned in this unit.

Mini Scrapbook

Choose an important experience. Make a scrapbook page with photos, souvenirs, other things you have kept, or just a list of memories.

A **Read.** A student is explaining his scrapbook page about a house guest. Have you ever had an interesting house guest?

A Wonderful Week with Kris

**Kris Heinlich
Berlin, Germany**
He was our guest.

A high school student from Germany stayed in our house for one week.

Places We Took Kris

Kris and me

My family took him to many places. He loved Adventure Park.

Adventureland Park Admit
Adventureland Park Admit One: July 28

A baseball game at Lincoln Stadium

When we said goodbye at the airport, he said, "You're my brother."

Adventureland Park

Hi Joey,
I want to thank you and your family for taking care of me. That was a great week. You should come to Germany sometime. You can stay in my house!
Kris

"You're my brother."
his goodbye words

A Letter He Sent Me

B Write. Choose an important experience for your scrapbook.

My important experience: _____

Things I could put on my scrapbook page (Check [✔] three or more items):

☐ photos   ☐ pictures from the Internet

☐ a schedule   ☐ a used ticket

☐ a souvenir   ☐ words I remember

☐ names of people   ☐ names of places

☐ a drawing   ☐ memos or letters

C Make. Create your scrapbook page. Follow these instructions:

1. Choose at least three things for your scrapbook.

2. Write a title on a large sheet of paper.

3. Paste, draw, or write the things you prepared on the paper.

4. Write a short description under each item.

D Write. Write a couple of sentences to tell your classmates what your important experience was.

_____

_____

Example:
Last year, a high school student from Germany stayed with my family for one week. His name was Kris, and we became good friends. It was a great experience.

E Speak. Show your scrapbook to your classmates. Tell them about the experience and they will ask questions.

Example:
A: How old was Kris?
B: Seventeen.
A: Uh-huh. And what's this?
B: Oh. It's a ticket from Adventureland Park.

An Amazing Trip 10

Challenge Preview

Unit Challenge

▸ Design a three-day tour.
▸ Tell other students about it.

A **Write.** Which tours are the most interesting? Number them from 1 (most interesting) to 4 (least interesting).

☐ a homestay on a ranch in Texas

☐ a cruise to New Zealand

☐ a shopping tour in Paris

☐ a guided tour of Egypt

B 🔘 **19** **Write and listen.** Ethan is telling Yumi about a tour he planned. Write *a*, *the*, or ✗ (for no article) to complete the conversation. Then listen to check your answers.

Ethan: On this tour, you'll learn how to play **soccer**.

Yumi: Oh good, I like _____ **soccer**.

Ethan: _____ tour is three days long.

Yumi: Uh-huh.

Ethan: On the first day, you'll go to **Los Angeles**. You'll meet **David Beckham**, and **he'll** give you _____ **soccer** lesson.

Yumi: **David Beckham**?

Ethan: Yes, **David Beckham**. **He's** _____ famous **soccer** player.

Superstar Training Tour

C **Speak.** Now practice the conversation with a partner. Then change the words in red to talk about a sport and sports person you know.

72

Working on Language ▶ Talking About Plans

> On this tour,   you**'ll go** to Spain.
> On the first day,   you**'ll see** a bullfight.
> After that,   you**'ll go** to a castle, but you **won't go** inside.

A   **Write.** Fill in the verbs. Use the correct verb tense: past, present, or future with *will*.

I (get) _____got_____ an e-mail this morning. Tomorrow, our class (go) _____will go_____ on a hike in Washington Park. I (bring) _____ my sister. After the hike, we (have) _____ a picnic. I (want) _____ to make sandwiches for everyone today, so yesterday I (buy) _____ some ham and bread. Tonight I (make) _____ the sandwiches, and tomorrow I (give) _____ them to my classmates.

B   **Write and speak.** Plan a birthday party for someone in your class. Use *will* to talk about your plan. Then discuss it with other students.

Party Ideas:

Level Up!
See page 121.

1. This is my plan for _____'s birthday party.

2. Before the party, we'll _____.

3. At the start of the party, _____.

4. After that, _____.

5. Later, _____.

6. After the party, _____.

Communicate ▶ Making a Travel Plan

A **Write.** You have $700 to plan a short trip to Paris. What do you want to do with your money? Make your travel plan and budget. Check [✔] one choice for each.

Travel from London to Paris . . .

☐ $100   by bus, 4 hours
☐ $150   by train, 2 hours
☐ $200   by plane, 1 hour

Stay . . .

☐ $100   in a homestay in a nearby town
☐ $150   in an old hotel near the city
☐ $300   in a nice hotel downtown

Go sightseeing . . .

☐ $0   on your own with a map
☐ $50   on a bus tour with a group
☐ $200   by car with a private guide

Eat . . .

☐ $30   in fast food restaurants
☐ $100   in inexpensive French cafés
☐ $200   in famous French restaurants

At night, go . . .

☐ $0   for a walk along the Seine River
☐ $100   on a cruise down the Seine River
☐ $200   to a dance show at the Moulin Rouge

How will you use the rest of your money?
(Fill in the amounts.)

$_____ to buy souvenirs for friends

$_____ to take French lessons

$_____

$_____

Useful Expressions

That sounds expensive.
That sounds reasonable.
That doesn't sound very comfortable.

B **Speak.** Interview some classmates about their travel plans. Who is the most similar to you?

Example:

A: How will you go to Paris?
B: I'll go by plane.
A: Why? That sounds expensive.
B: Because I hate long trips.

Working on Fluency ▶ Showing You Are Listening

A 🔘 **20** **Listen.** A tour guide is explaining a tour of London to a tourist. Number the pictures from 1 to 4 in the order you hear them.

B 🔘 **20** **Listen again.** The tourist makes sounds and short comments as she listens. Circle the four she uses.

Guide: Welcome to London. Now, let me tell you about today's plan. At nine a.m. . . . .

Tourist: Uh-huh.

Guide: . . . we will meet in the lobby.

> Right.   OK.   Yeah?   Sure.   Oh, nice.   Uh-huh.

💡 Critical Thinking

These phrases can also be said in a way to show that you don't believe something. Practice these conversations.

He says he will get 100 points on the test.

- Uh-huh. (*you think so*)
- Uhhh-huhhh. (*you don't think so*)

C **Speak.** Tell your partner about one of the topics below. Your partner will use phrases like those above as you speak.

- ▶ what I had for dinner last night
- ▶ my favorite places near my home
- ▶ what I usually do on New Year's Day
- ▶ the people in my family

Example:

A: Last night, I had dinner in a Chinese restaurant.

B: Uh-huh.

A: I had, um, fried rice, egg soup . . .

B: Right.

Challenge

Design a fantastic vacation and hold a travel fair. Try to get as many students to join your tour as possible.

A Check. Check [✔] the tour advertisement you like the most.

Go to California and take soccer lessons from a great player.

Travel by time machine to the Mongol Empire. Ride with Genghis Khan as he conquers the world.

Take a rocket trip to the moon. Walk on the moon and take photos.

B Write. Think of another interesting tour and make a plan for it. Write activities for each day, like the example in the chart.

	Example: Superstar Training Tour	Your tour:
Day 1	You'll: • go to Los Angeles. • meet David Beckham. • get a soccer lesson.	
Day 2	You'll: • practice soccer. • have a party.	
Day 3	You'll: • play a soccer game in a big stadium with other famous players.	

C **Write and draw.** Make an advertisement for your tour on a piece of paper. Include the following:

▸ the name of the tour at the top
▸ a catch phrase to promote it
▸ the schedule for each day

D **Speak.** Tell at least three other students about your tour.

Example:

A: Do you want to hear about my Superstar Training Tour?

B: It's a soccer tour?

A: Uh-huh. You'll go to California, and you'll take soccer lessons from a great player . . .

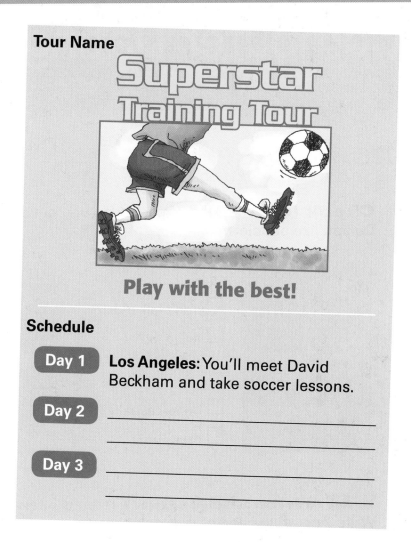

Tour Name

Superstar Training Tour

Play with the best!

Schedule

Day 1 **Los Angeles:** You'll meet David Beckham and take soccer lessons.

Day 2 _____

_____

Day 3 _____

_____

E **Choose.** Put a piece of paper with "Tour Sign-up Sheet" on it next to your tour advertisement. Then go to one or more tours that you liked and sign up. Write your name and a comment about the tour.

Tour Sign-up Sheet

Robert Martinez – I really want to meet David Beckham.

I'm his biggest fan!

Reflection Time

Write useful words and ideas you learned in this unit.

Challenge Preview

Unit Challenge
▸ Interview a classmate.
▸ Describe a perfect partner for him or her.

A Check [✓]. What kind of people do you get along with? Do you like people who . . .

- ☐ don't talk much?
- ☐ talk a lot?

- ☐ dress casually?
- ☐ dress up?

- ☐ like outdoor activities?
- ☐ like indoor activities?

- ☐ like parties?
- ☐ like doing things at home?

B 🔘 **21 Write and listen.** Kirsten is interviewing James about his ideal partner. Write *?* or *.* at the end of the sentences to complete the conversation. Then listen to the dialog.

Kirsten:	Do you want a partner who **watches TV at night, or reads**___
James:	Hmm . . . I want a partner who **reads**___
Kirsten:	Like what, for example___
James:	Hmm. **Novels, magazines**, . . . anything really___
Kirsten:	What else about your partner's interests is important___
James:	I want a partner who **likes to travel**___

C Speak. Now practice the conversation with a partner. Then change the words in red to talk about this picture.

▸ likes indoor or outdoor activities
▸ likes outdoor activities
▸ camping, hiking
▸ likes to talk

Working on Language ▶ Describing People You Like

Describing Oneself	Describing Others
I'm interested in sports.	I like **people who are** interested in sports.
I don't worry much about fashion.	I like **people who don't worry** much about fashion.
I like to help **my** parents.	I like **people who like** to help **their** parents.

A **Write.** Complete the sentences.

"I love shopping."

"I work hard."

"I don't tell lies."

"I'm interested in art."

"I help my parents"

1. "I like people who_____."

2. "I like people who_____."

3. "_____"

4. "_____"

5. "_____"

B **Write and speak.** Write two sentences about the kind of people you like. Then discuss them with a classmate.

1. _____

2. _____

Example:
A: What kind of people do you like?
B: I really like people who are funny. How about you?
A: Me too!

Level Up!
See page 122.

Computer Dating Service   **79**

Communicate ▶ What Do You Prefer?

A **Write.** Add three more questions to the questionnaire. Then complete the questionnaire with your own information.

How Well Do You Know Yourself?

Are you someone who likes to _____ or _____?   **Your answers**

1. stay at home	go out	
2. listen to music	watch TV	
3. send email	talk on the phone	
4. make money	have free time	
5.		
6.		
7.		

B **Speak and write.** Ask three partners the questions on your questionnaire. Write down their answers. Who is the most like you?

Partner 1	Partner 2	Partner 3

Example:
A: Do you prefer to stay at home or to go out?
B: I like to go out. How about you?
A: Not me. I like to stay at home.

Useful Expressions

Me too.
Not me.
I don't really care.

Working on Fluency ▶ Asking for Specific Details

A 🔘 **22** **Write and listen.** Fill in the missing *Wh-* words. Then listen to check.

Michael: Hey Janet. I heard you quit your job.

Janet: Yeah, I had some problems with it.

Michael: Oh really? Like _____?

Janet: Well, some people were really hard to get along with.

Michael: Umm. Like _____, for example?

Janet: Well, my boss. He wasn't very nice. He made me travel a lot.

Michael: Like _____, for example?

Janet: To other cities, like St. Louis, Cleveland, Seattle. I was just never home! It was terrible!

B **Write.** Make follow-up questions for each statement.

Example: I love desserts. _____Like what, for example?_____

1. I want to go out tonight. _____

2. I like my classmates. _____

3. I want to eat Italian food. _____

4. I want to go abroad some day. _____

5. I like nice people. _____

C **Speak.** Say the sentences in Activity B to a partner. Your partner will ask for more information. Answer with something that is true for you.

Example:

A: I love desserts.

B: Like what, for example?

A: My favorite is chocolate ice cream.

💡 Critical Thinking

Think about how to use follow-up questions. Check the statements that can be followed by "like what?" then add one more.

☐ There are some things I have to do today.

☐ I love my goldfish.

☐ I ate a ham sandwich.

☐ I want to eat something spicy.

Your idea: _____

_____

Challenge

Design and give an interview to find out what kind of person your partner likes. (Your partner can give his or her answers, or pretend to be a famous person.) Then find a perfect computer date for your partner.

A Write. As a class, brainstorm interview questions like the examples in the chart in Activity B. Write your favorite questions in the interview chart.

B Speak and write. Interview a partner and take notes on the answers.

INTERVIEW CHART	
Do you . . .	**Your Partner's Answers**
Interests **1.** want a partner who likes sports, or who likes to study? **2.** _____ ? **3.** _____ ? **4.** What else about your partner's interests is important?	
Personality **1.** want a partner who is quiet and shy, or active and outgoing? **2.** _____ ? **3.** _____ ? **4.** What else about your partner's personality is important?	
Looks **1.** like long hair or short hair? **2.** _____ ? **3.** _____ ? **4.** What else about your partner's looks is important?	
What else is important to you?	

C Write. Find a computer date that fits your partner. Be creative.

Computer Dating Services found your perfect partner!

Name: _____ Age: _____

Job: _____

Hobbies and Interests:

- _____
- _____
- _____

(Draw or paste a picture here.)

On weekends, your computer date likes to do these things:

_____

Personality: Your computer date is a _____ person.
For example, _____

Dream:
Someday, your computer date wants to _____
_____

D Speak. Tell your classmate about his or her computer date.

Example:

A: Your partner's name is Bart Pitt. He is 32 years old, and he loves soccer.

B: He loves to play soccer?

A: Yes, and baseball too.

Reflection Time

Write useful words and ideas you learned in this unit.

Talent Show

Challenge Preview

Unit Challenge
▸ Show your class something unusual you can do.
▸ Tell them how you learned it.
▸ Teach them how to do it.

A **Check [✓].** Which of these things can you do?

☐ **Do** a card trick.

☐ **Make** a paper airplane.

☐ **Touch** your nose with your tongue.

☐ **Play** an instrument.

☐ **Say** "I love you" in four languages.

B 🔘 23 **Write and listen.** James is showing the class how to do a card trick. Write *a* or *the* to complete the conversation. Then listen to check your answers.

James: Let me show you _____ card trick. **Sang-mi**, can you **help** me?

Sang-mi: Sure. What should I do?

James: Take _____ card. **Show** everyone, but not me.

Sang-mi: OK. Got it. Show everyone, but not you.

James: **Good.** Now, **put** _____ card back.

Sang-mi: Like this?

James: **Yeah.** Next, I do this and this. . . . Is this _____ card?

Sang-mi: Yes. That's amazing!

C **Speak.** Practice the conversation with a partner. Then practice the conversation again, using the words *please* and *thank you* to make the conversation more polite.

Working on Language ▶ Giving Instructions

Instruction	More Information
This is how to make a floating hot dog.	
First, **do** this with your fingers.	
Now, **look** past your fingers at something else.	
Then, **move** your fingers apart a little, like this.	You can see a hot dog.

First,    **Now,**    **Then,**

A Match. Connect the sentence halves with lines.

1. This is how to play cheek music.

First, do •   • with your finger.

Then, hit your cheek •   • your mouth a little. You can play a song.

Now, open and close •   • this with your mouth.

2. This is how to say "I like you" in American Sign Language.

First, point •   • at someone else.

Then, do •   • at yourself. It means "I."

Now, point •   • this. You are pulling your heart.

Level Up!
See page 123.

B Write and speak. Explain how to use a pay phone. Practice with a partner.

This is how to use a pay phone.

 pick up

First, _____

 put in

_____

 push

_____

Communicate ▶ Can You . . . ?

A **Check [✓].** What can you do? Check the things you can do. Then add your own idea.

☐ play tennis

☐ do a magic trick

☐ make a pizza

☐ ride a skateboard

☐ play chess

☐ play the piano

☐ say something in Spanish

SE HABLA ESPAÑOL

Your Idea!

B **Speak and write.** Ask other students questions about what they can do. Write one interesting piece of information for each person you interview.

Example:

A: Can you play tennis?
B: Yes, but I'm not very good at it.
A: Who taught you how to play?
B: My younger brother.

Useful Expressions
Just a little.
I'm not very good at it.
Sure I can.

Kirsten: can play tennis

Luis: can do a card trick

A 🔘 **24** **Listen.** Lisa is telling Marissa, her younger sister, how to put on lipstick. Number the pictures to show the order.

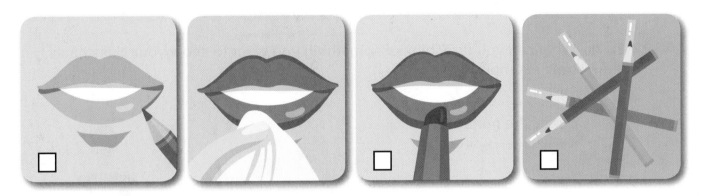

B **Listen again and write.** What does Marissa ask to check the following directions? Write the questions.

1. Choose a lip liner.   <u>Like this one?</u>

2. Draw lines around your lips.   <u>   </u>

3. Put lipstick on your lips.   <u>   </u>

4. Use a tissue like this.   <u>   </u>

C **Speak.** Tell your partner to do things with his or her hands. Your partner will do them and check your instructions.

Example:
A: Put your hand on your head.
B: Like this?
A: Yes. Now put your finger on your nose.
B: Is this right?
A: No. Just one finger.

💡 **Critical Thinking**

Think about how the way you say something changes its meaning. Practice this dialog:

A: Write your name here.

B: Like this? (*say it like you are just checking*)

A: No, hold your pen with both hands.

B: Like this? (*say it like you don't believe this is right*)

Challenge

Show other students something you can do. Then tell them how you learned it. Try to teach them how to do it.

A **Think.** What can you do? Think of something you want to show your classmates. Here are some examples.

play the guitar

wiggle your ears

dance

paint a picture

stand on your head

B **Prepare.** Practice what you will do. Also, write what you will say.

Example:

Let me show you how to play the guitar. I learned how to play when I was in high school. A friend taught me.

This is how to do it.

1. Hold the guitar like this.

2. Put your hand right here.

3. Do this with your left hand. And then . . .

C Present. Follow these instructions.

1. Get some pieces of paper to write comments on.

2. Do something interesting in front of the class.

Now, do this. Please remember the top card.

3. Explain how you learned it and how to do it.

James,

That was amazing. Please show me how to do it again after class.

Rey

4. Your classmates will give you comments.

Presentation Tip

When you're not using your hands, let them fall naturally to your sides. Don't hold them in front of you, or behind you.

Reflection Time

Write useful words and ideas you learned in this unit.

Personal Progress Bookmark

What things can you say in English now that you couldn't say before taking this class? What else did you learn? Make a bookmark showing your progress. Then, have your classmates sign it.

A **Read.** This student is talking about her progress in English. Are any of these changes true for you too?

Your progress

> I learned the expression, "You're kidding!" in this class. I love it. These are "my words" now.

Basic English 101
May 2012

Your classmates' signatures

I learned:
- "You're kidding!"
- "How do you spell that?"
- "Ancestor"
- How to talk about my family

> I couldn't talk about my family in English before. Now, I think I can.

I also:
- Made many friends
- Like English better now
- Decided to study English more

Sang Me Kim

Etham
Let's get together!

James Lin-
Your Friend

Yumi Ito

Kim Lang
I love you!

Rey Diaz

> I made many good friends in this class. We'll stay in touch after this class ends.

B Reflect. Go back through this student book, especially the Reflection Time boxes. What do you remember about the course? Write your ideas:

Your favorite expressions:

You're kidding! _____ _____
_____ _____
_____ _____
_____ _____

Other experiences:

I made good friends. _____ _____
_____ _____
_____ _____
_____ _____

C Make. Fold a sheet of paper to make a bookmark, and tape or glue it closed. Then write these things on the front side.

▸ the name of the class
▸ the date
▸ your favorite expressions
▸ other experiences

D Speak. Tell other students what you learned in class and how you changed.

Example:

I learned "You're kidding!" Do you like those words? I do. I feel like they're mine.

E Write. Pass your bookmarks around. Your classmates will sign their names on the back. Then make a hole in the top and add a string. Now you have a bookmark to remember your class!

Basic English 101
May 2012

I learned:
• "You're kidding!"
• "How do you spell that?"
• "Ancestor"
• How to talk about my family

I also:
• Made many friends
• Like English better now
• Decided to study English more

Unit 8: Challenge

Student B

A **Speak.** These are pictures of Betty's family members. Ask questions to find out each person's name and relationship to Betty.

Example:

Student B: Who's Julie?

Student A: She's Betty's grandmother.

Student B: What's her husband's name?

Student A: William.

Student B: How do you spell that?

Student A: W-I-L-L-I-A-M.

♂ **Name:** _____
Betty's: _____
Job: _____

♀ **Name:** _Julie_____
Betty's: _grandmother_
Job: _____
Children's Names:
1. _____
2. _____

♂ **Name:** _____
Betty's: _____
Job: _____

♀ **Name:** _____
Betty's: _____
Job: _____
Children's Names:
1. _____
2. _____

♂ **Name:** _____
Betty's: _____
Job: _____

♂ **Name:** _____
Betty's: _____
Job: _____

♀ **Name:** _____
Betty's: _____
Job: _____

♂ **Name:** _____
Betty's: _____
Age: _____

♂ **Name:** _____
Betty's: _____
Age: _____

♀ **Name:** _____
Betty's: _____
Age: _____

B **Speak.** This is John's family tree. First complete the relationship words. Then your partner (Student A) will ask questions about John's family members.

Example:

Student A: Does John have a relative who's a police officer?

Student A: How are they related?

Student B: Yes. His name is Billy.

Student B: He's John's grandfather.

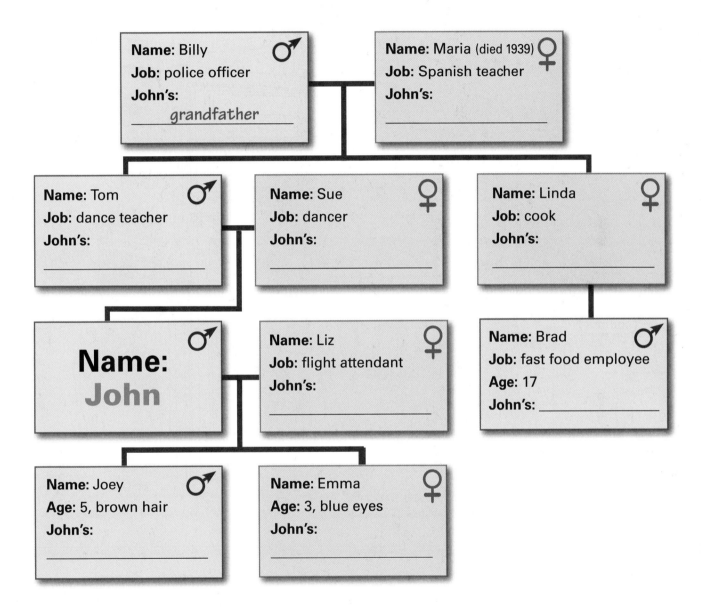

Name: Billy ♂
Job: police officer
John's:
_____grandfather_____

Name: Maria (died 1939) ♀
Job: Spanish teacher
John's:
_____

Name: Tom ♂
Job: dance teacher
John's:
_____

Name: Sue ♀
Job: dancer
John's:
_____

Name: Linda ♀
Job: cook
John's:
_____

Name:
John ♂

Name: Liz ♀
Job: flight attendant
John's:
_____

Name: Brad ♂
Job: fast food employee
Age: 17
John's: _____

Name: Joey ♂
Age: 5, brown hair
John's:
_____

Name: Emma ♀
Age: 3, blue eyes
John's:
_____

C **Speak.** John and Betty have one mysterious relative who is the same person! Can you find that person? If so, try to figure out what happened in his or her life.

Reflection Time

Write useful words and ideas you learned in this unit.

Unit 4: Challenge

Student B
What's for dinner? After Freddy Cooked Dinner

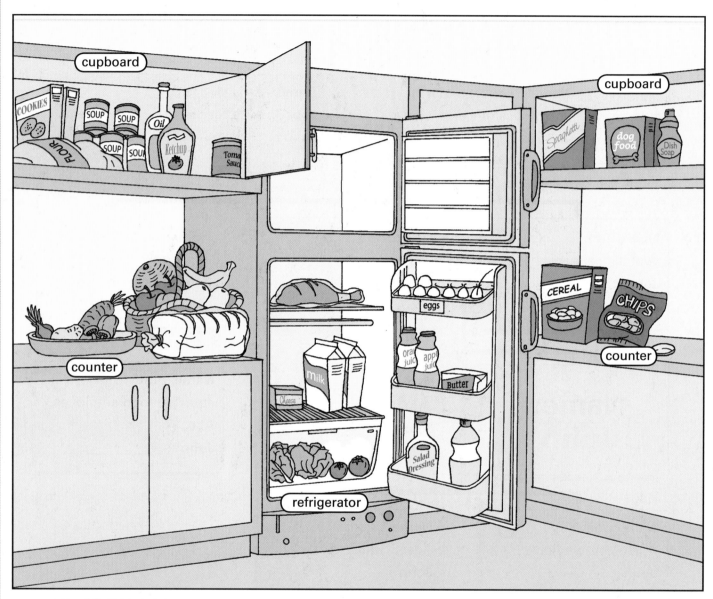

What did Freddy use?		What did Freddy make for dinner?
1. _____	5. _____	
2. _____	6. _____	
3. _____	7. _____	
4. _____	8. _____	

Reflection Time

Write useful words and ideas you learned in this unit.

AUDIO SCRIPTS

Unit 1 **Challenge Preview**

Rey: Hi. I'm Reynaldo Diaz.
Yumi: Hi, Reynaldo. I'm Yumi Ito.
Rey: It's nice to meet you. Please, call me Rey.

Yumi: Call me Yumi. All my friends do.
Rey: OK, Yumi. Please tell me about your poster. What's this?
Yumi: It's my hometown. I'm from Tokyo.

 Unit 1 **Working on Fluency**

Cathy: That's Jon. He is really cool.
Sarah: Well, I don't know . . .
Cathy: Yeah, I love his hairstyle.
Sarah: Hmm.

Cathy: That's Susanna. She looks athletic.
Sarah: Yes, I think so too. She's wearing jogging pants.
Cathy: Yeah, and running shoes . . .

Cathy: And there's Ben. He's so friendly.
Sarah: Yeah . . . really.
Cathy: He's got a great smile.

Cathy: And Keri, she's so fashionable.
Sarah: Are you kidding? Blue shoes and a purple top?
Cathy: Yeah. It's really different! I love it!

Spoken English: Table of Contents

When speaking, native speakers of American English often change the way they pronounce certain phrases. In this section, there are examples of:

1. Meet you ▶ "Meechu"
2. Strong Syllables
3. Stressing Important Words
4. Stressed Words in Sentences
5. Linking Words with *y*
6. Linking Words with *s* and *z*

7. Have to ▶ "Hafta"
8. Asking How to Spell Words
9. Stress Patterns in Compound Nouns
10. Linking Words with *t* and *d*
11. Want a ▶ "Wanna"
12. Linking Words with *w*

Spoken English: Meet you ▶ "Meechu"

A. Listen to this item on the audio CD.

It's nice to **meet you**. Please call me Rey.

B. Now practice these sentences:

1. It's nice to <u>meet you</u> too, Rey.
2. I'm happy to <u>meet you</u>, too.
3. I can't <u>meet you</u> today.
4. I can <u>meet you</u> tomorrow.

---

3 Unit 2 **Challenge Preview**

Kirsten:	Do you like ice cream?
James:	Yes, I do. I love it! How about you?
Kirsten:	I like it too. What kind of ice cream do you like?
James:	Strawberry. It's my favorite. Do you like strawberry ice cream, too?
Kirsten:	No, I don't. I can't stand it!

 4 Unit 2 **Working on Fluency**

Susanna:	Do you like shopping?
Ben:	I love shopping! How about you?
Susanna:	Me, too. I go shopping almost every day.
Ben:	Oh really? Where do you like to shop?
Susanna:	I'm crazy about the mall. How about you?
Ben:	Not me. I can't stand the mall.
Susanna:	Really? I can't stand shopping online. How about you?
Ben:	Me neither. I use my computer to play games, not shop!

Spoken English: Strong Syllables

A. Listen to this exchange on the audio CD.

Kirsten:	What kind of ice cream do you like?
James:	**Straw**berry. It's my **fa**vorite. Do you like **straw**berry ice cream, too?

B. Now practice these sentences.

1. I like <u>vanilla</u> ice cream.
2. My <u>favorite</u> <u>flavor</u> is <u>chocolate</u>.
3. I like <u>banana</u> ice cream.
4. He likes <u>blueberry</u> <u>yogurt</u>.

Unit 3   Challenge Preview

Ethan: Tell me about your ideal town. Who lives next to you?

Sang-mi: My grandmother.

Ethan: Does she live on the right or on the left?

Sang-mi: She's on the right.

Ethan: Okay. What are some other places in your town?

Sang-mi: Well, there's a convenience store across from my house.

Ethan: A convenience store? That's handy.

Unit 3   Working on Fluency

Yumi: Hi Rey. Where are you?

Rey: I'm at the game center.

Yumi: The game center? Where's that?

Rey: It's across from the pizza place.

Yumi: Across from the pizza place?

Rey: Yeah, Harpo's Pizza.

Yumi: Okay. Anyway, come to the movie theater, and hurry! The movie starts in ten minutes!

Rey: The movie theater? In ten minutes?

Yumi: Yes, the movie theater. We have a date. Remember?

Rey: Oh . . . um . . . of course! See you soon.

Spoken English: Stressing Important Words

A. Listen to this exchange on the audio CD.

Ethan: Does she live on the **right** or on the **left**?

Sang-mi: She's on the **right**.

B. Now practice these questions and answers.

1. **Q:** Does she live in a <u>big</u> house or a <u>small</u> house?

   A: She lives in a <u>small</u> house.

2. **Q:** Do you live near the <u>school</u> or near the <u>park</u>?

   A: I live near the <u>park</u>.

3. **Q:** Is the convenience store on the <u>right</u> or on the <u>left</u>?

   A: It's on the <u>left</u>.

7 Unit 4   **Challenge Preview**

James: Look at the kitchen counter on the left.

Yumi: On the left?

James: Yes, that's right. How many onions are there?

Yumi: In my picture, there are three onions.

James: There's only one onion in my picture.

Yumi: So, he used two of the onions!

8 Unit 4   **Working on Fluency**

Lauren: Hello?

Adam: Hey Lauren, I'm at the store. What do we need?

Lauren: Hmm. Let me check in the kitchen. Let's see . . . we need two cartons of eggs, and . . .

Adam: Wait. Two cartons of eggs?

Lauren: Yes, two. Also buy four bags of flour. And . . .

Adam: Hang on. Four?

Lauren: Yes. And buy three packs of butter, and let's see . . .

Adam: Excuse me? Why so many?

Lauren: So I can make three cakes for the birthday party!

Spoken English: Stressed Words in Sentences

A. Listen to this exchange on the audio CD.

Yumi: In **my** picture, there are **three** onions.

James: There is only **one** onion in **my** picture.

B. Now practice these sentences.

1. In <u>my</u> house, there are <u>three</u> TVs.
2. In <u>your</u> house, there are <u>four</u> bedrooms. In <u>my</u> house, there are <u>three</u> bedrooms.
3. There are <u>five</u> eggs and <u>four</u> onions, not <u>five</u> onions and <u>four</u> eggs.
4. In <u>my</u> picture, there are <u>two</u> tomatoes. In <u>your</u> picture, there is <u>one</u> tomato.

Kirsten:	My holiday is Pajama Day. It's on May 9.
James:	I see. So how do you celebrate it?
Kirsten:	On this day, we wear our pajamas everywhere.
James:	Uh, really? Do you wear your pajamas to school?
Kirsten:	Yes. At home, at school, everywhere!
James:	Oh, I see. Anything else?
Kirsten:	Uh-huh. At midnight, we have a pajama party!

 10 **Unit 5** **Working on Fluency**

James:	What's your favorite holiday, Aoy?
Aoy:	My favorite holiday? Hmm. I guess it's Songkran.
James:	Songkran? What's that?
Aoy:	It's the Thai New Year. Some people call it the . . . um . . . Water Festival.
James:	Oh right. So, uh . . . how do you celebrate it?
Aoy:	Well . . . I always go back to . . . to my hometown, Chiang Mai . . . and . . . uh . . . I meet my family.
James:	Um . . . anything else?
Aoy:	Let's see . . . there are parades, and well . . . people . . . uh . . . throw water on each other. Everyone gets really wet. It's fun!

> **Spoken English:** Linking Words with *y*
>
> **A.** Listen to this sentence on the audio CD.
>
> **Kirsten:** My **holiday is** Pajama Day. It's on May 9.
>
> **B.** Now practice these sentences.
> 1. My <u>birthday is</u> on December 9.
> 2. My favorite <u>holiday is</u> Halloween.
> 3. <u>Why is</u> your favorite holiday Halloween?
> 4. <u>Friday is</u> my favorite day of the week.

Unit 6 — Challenge Preview

Sang-mi:	My award is for the receptionist.
Rey:	The receptionist? Does she work in the main office?
Sang-mi:	Yes. She works in the main office, but I don't know her name.
Rey:	So, why her?
Sang-Mi:	Well, she always smiles and says "hello."
Rey:	Really? She sounds friendly.

 Unit 6 — Working on Fluency

Peggy:	Sometimes, my boss takes us to restaurants.
Don:	He sounds nice.
Peggy:	Yes, he is. I really appreciate him. Last month, we went to a movie together too.
Don:	Really? That sounds fun.
Peggy:	And today, he gave me a birthday present, a new car. I love it!
Don:	A car? From your boss? That sounds strange.
Peggy:	No, not at all . . . because . . . He's my father too!
Don:	Oh. I see!

Spoken English: Linking words with *s* and *z*

A. Listen to these items on the audio CD.

Sang-mi:	Yes, she **works in** Mr. Lee's office. [s-sound]
Rey:	Well, she always **smiles and** says "hello." [z-sound]

B. Now practice these sentences.

1. He <u>always eats at</u> home.
2. She <u>sounds strange</u>.
3. That <u>sounds interesting</u>.
4. He <u>lives in</u> America and <u>works at</u> a big company.

13 Unit 7 Challenge Preview

Kirsten: What is the job?
Ethan: Zoo employee.
Kirsten: What do I have to do?
Ethan: Well, first, you have to wash the elephants. Then you have to feed the lions.

Kirsten: You're kidding! It sounds like a really dangerous job.
Ethan: You're right. It is.

14 Unit 7 Working on Fluency

Man: I have to tell you about my new job. It's amazing. I am a bed tester!
Woman: A what?
Man: A bed tester. I test new beds for a bed company. I lie down in a bed and tell my boss how it feels.
Woman: You're kidding!

Man: No. I'm serious. And it's not just for a few minutes. I have to stay in bed for two hours.
Woman: I can't believe it!
Man: And . . . they pay me more money than my other job does.
Woman: No. Really?
Man: Yes. Really!

Spoken English: Have to ▶ "Hafta"

A. Listen to this exchange on the audio CD.

Kirsten: What do I **have to** do?
Ethan: Well, first, you **have to** wash the elephants. Then you **have to** feed the lions.

B. Now practice these sentences.

1. What do you <u>have to</u> do at your job?
2. I <u>have to</u> wash the dishes and I <u>have to</u> clean the tables.
3. I <u>have to</u> do a lot of homework tonight.
4. What do you <u>have to</u> do tonight?

Unit 8   Challenge Preview

Sang-mi: I have some old pictures of John's family. Is one of his relatives a police officer?
Rey: Yes. His name is Billy.
Sang-mi: How do you spell that?

Rey: B-I-L-L-Y. Did you get that?
Sang-mi: Yes, thanks. Um. How are they related?
Rey: He's his grandfather.
Sang-mi: So, he's his grandfather. I see.

 Unit 8   Working on Fluency

Lawyer: Are you Lisa Jones? Ben Jones' great-granddaughter?
Woman: Yes, why?
Lawyer: I have some good news for you. Ben Jones had a house in England. It's yours now.
Woman: Sorry. I don't understand.

Lawyer: Ben died 50 years ago. He had a huge house in England. Now the castle is yours.
Woman: Did you say "castle?"
Lawyer: Yes. Appleby Castle is yours!
Woman: Apple . . . ? How do you spell that?
Lawyer: A-P-P-L-E-B-Y. It's a lovely home . . .

Spoken English: Asking How to Spell Words

A. Listen to this exchange on the audio CD. Notice the intonation.

Sang-mi: How do you spell that?
Rey: B-I-L-L-Y.

B. Now practice these questions and answers.

1. **Q:** How do you spell *related*?
   A: R-E-L-A-T-E-D
2. **Q:** How do you spell *relative*?
   A: R-E-L-A-T-I-V-E
3. **Q:** Your name is *Marcus*? How do you spell that?
   A: M-A-R-C-U-S

17 Unit 9   Challenge Preview

Yumi: What's this?

James: When I was a high school student, I was on the soccer team. I really loved it.

Yumi: The soccer team? Wow! That's cool.

James: Yeah, it was. But in one game, I suddenly got hit in the face with the ball.

Yumi: Oh, that's terrible. Were you hurt?

James: Yes, a little bit, but we still won!

18 Unit 9   Working on Fluency

Ted: Guess what? Recently, I was in an accident.

Joy: What happened?

Ted: Ali gave Ethan and me a ride on the back of his bicycle; three of us rode on one bicycle!

Joy: Was it fun?

Ted: Yeah, it was, but then he went onto a busy street. There were cars all around us.

Joy: Were you scared?

Ted: Of course. And then, BAM! We hit a car.

Joy: Oh dear. Was anyone hurt?

Ted: No, but we broke the mirror on the car.

Joy: Was the driver angry?

Ted: Of course. He shouted at Ali. We were all really embarrassed!

Spoken English: Stress Patterns in Compound Nouns

A. Listen to this exchange on the audio CD.

James: When I was a **high school** student, I was on the **soccer team**. I really loved it.

Yumi: The **soccer team**? Wow! That's cool!

B. Now practice these sentences.

1. When I was a junior high school student, I was on the debate team.

2. I was in the city tennis club championship a few years ago.

3. When I was an elementary school student, I won the school speech contest.

4. I got my driver's license when I was a high school student.

19 Unit 10 **Challenge Preview**

Ethan: On this tour, you'll learn how to play soccer.
Yumi: Oh good, I like soccer.
Ethan: The tour is three days long.
Yumi: Uh-huh.

Ethan: On the first day, you'll go to Los Angeles. You'll meet David Beckham, and he'll give you a soccer lesson.
Yumi: David Beckham?
Ethan: Yes, David Beckham. He's a famous soccer player.

 20 Unit 10 **Working on Fluency**

Guide: Welcome to London. Now, let me tell you about today's plan. At nine a.m. . . .
Tourist: Uh huh.
Guide: . . . we will meet in the lobby.
Tourist: OK.
Guide: Then we'll get on a bus, you know, one of those old style buses with two floors of seats and we will then take a tour of the downtown area.

Tourist: Oh, nice.
Guide: We'll see Big Ben, you know, that big clock? And um . . .
Tourist: Yeah?
Guide: . . . then, the Tower Bridge.
Tourist: Hmm. That sounds like fun.

Spoken English: Linking Words with *t* and *d*

A. Listen to these items on the audio CD.
On the **first day**, you'll go to Los Angeles. You'll **meet David** Beckham, . . .

B. Now practice these sentences.
1. On, the <u>last day</u>, you'll go to a concert.
2. You <u>can't take</u> more than one suitcase.
3. <u>Don't drink</u> any water there.
4. You'll <u>find ten</u> art shops <u>and two</u> music shops.

Kirsten: Do you want a partner who watches TV at night, or reads?

James: Hmm . . . I want a partner who reads.

Kirsten: Like what, for example?

James: Hmm. Novels, magazines, . . . anything, really.

Kirsten: What else about your partner's interests is important?

James: I want a partner who likes to travel.

 Unit 11 Working on Fluency

Michael: Hey Janet. I heard you quit your job.

Janet: Yeah, I had some problems with it.

Michael: Oh really? Like what?

Janet: Well, some people were really hard to get along with.

Michael: Umm . . . Like who, for example?

Janet: Well, my boss. He wasn't very nice. He made me travel a lot.

Michael: Like where, for example?

Janet: To other cities, like St. Louis, Cleveland, Seattle. I was just never home! It was terrible!

Spoken English: Want a ▶ "Wanna"

A. Listen to these items on the audio CD.

Q: Do you **want a** partner who watches TV at night, or reads?

A: Hmm . . . I **want a** partner who reads.

A: I **want a** partner who likes to travel.

B. Now practice these sentences.

1. Do you <u>want a</u> partner who likes to dance?

2. I <u>want a</u> partner who likes to dance.

3. Do you <u>want a</u> partner who is funny, or do you <u>want a</u> partner who is serious?

4. I <u>want a</u> partner who is funny. I don't <u>want a</u> partner who's serious all the time.

23 Unit 12 **Challenge Preview**

James: Let me show you a card trick. Sang-mi, can you help me?

Sang-mi: Sure. What should I do?

James: Take a card. Show everyone, but not me.

Sang-mi: OK. Got it. Show everyone, but not you.

James: Good. Now, put the card back.

Sang-mi: Like this?

James: Yeah . . . Next, I do this and this . . . Is this the card?

Sang-mi: Yes. That's amazing!

 24 Unit 12 **Working on Fluency**

Lisa: OK, Marissa, first, choose a lip liner. It should be darker than your lipstick.

Marissa: Like this one?

Lisa: Yes. Now, draw lines around your lips, like this.

Marissa: Like this?

Lisa: No. Not like that. Just on the outside of your lip, like this. Now put lipstick on your lips, like this.

Marissa: Like this?

Lisa: Yes, like that. Now use a tissue like this.

Marissa: Is this right?

Lisa: Yes, perfect, Marissa. You look lovely.

Spoken English: Linking Words with *w*

A. Listen to this exchange on the audio CD.

James: Take a card. **Show everyone**, but not me.

Sang-mi: OK. Got it. **Show everyone**, but not you.

B. Now practice these sentences.

1. <u>Show us</u> the card you chose.
2. He's <u>slow at</u> everything he does.
3. Now I'll <u>show it</u> to everyone.
4. She's <u>now out</u> of the country.

When You Have Time

If you finish an activity in this unit before your classmates, try one of these.

A Do the quiz. Mark these sentences about you as 1 (not true), 2 (a little true), or 3 (very true).

1. _____ I hate to be alone.   _____ I love to be alone.

2. _____ I like to study or work.   _____ I don't like to study or work.

3. _____ I am neat and careful.   _____ I am not so careful, but creative.

4. _____ I am generally a happy person.   _____ I am generally a sad person.

5. _____ I am usually nervous around people.   _____ I am usually relaxed around people.

B Talk with a partner about your class.

1. Do you know anyone in this class? Who?

2. Who in this class do you want to get to know better?

3. Do you know anything about the teacher?

4. What do you want to learn in this class?

C Look at the chart. Then rewrite the sentences with contractions.

Level Up ▶ Contractions	
I am from Melbourne. **He is** from Sydney, but **he is not** an Australian. **We are not** athletic, but **we are** on the team. **You do not** like parties because **you are** shy.	**I'm** from Melbourne. **He's** from Sydney, but **he isn't** an Australian. **We aren't** athletic, but **we're** on the team. **You don't** like parties because **you're** shy.

1. She is talkative, but I am quiet.   _____

2. You are from London, but they are not.   _____

3. Mary is a singer, but she is not very good.   _____

4. They are always on time, so do not be late.   _____

If you finish an activity in this unit before your classmates, try one of these.

A Do you know what these sports are? In which country is each the most popular sport?

_____ Japan   _____ United States   _____ India   _____ Canada   _____ England

B Talk with a partner about things you don't like.

1. What's a song you can't stand?
2. What kind of food do you hate?
3. Are there any TV programs you can't stand?
4. What music groups don't you like?
5. Are there any sports you hate?

C Look at the chart. Then complete the answers with the correct pronoun.

Level Up ▸ Pronouns		
I like I don't like	**it** **him** **her** **them**	a lot. very much.
It **He** **She** **They**	is are	OK.

1. Do you like watching sports on TV?   No, I don't like _____ very much.
2. How about comedy shows?   _____ are OK.
3. Do you like pop songs?   Yes. I'm crazy about _____.
4. How about Lady Gaga?   _____ is OK.
5. Do you like hip-hop singers?   I like _____.
6. How about Jay-Z?   No. I can't stand _____.

If you finish an activity in this unit before your classmates, try one of these.

A Do the word search. Find nine names of buildings (some are new).

apartment
hotel
house
office
restaurant
school
station
store
supermarket

t	l	e	t	o	h	e	o	l	o
e	n	t	i	t	s	s	n	o	r
k	s	a	n	e	o	a	t	p	r
r	u	c	r	f	n	p	t	u	e
a	c	a	f	u	a	a	e	s	e
m	f	i	e	h	a	r	t	t	m
r	c	u	s	t	a	t	i	o	n
e	t	p	u	f	p	m	s	r	e
p	r	r	o	t	t	e	t	e	s
u	e	a	h	h	r	n	h	o	r
s	c	h	o	o	l	t	p	t	e

B Talk with a partner about your home.

1. Where do you live?

2. Is it an apartment, a house, or another kind of place?

3. What do you like about where you live?

4. What do you dislike about where you live?

C Look at the chart. Then fill in the missing prepositions in the story below.

Level Up ▶ Describing Locations

There's a bridge	**over**	the river.
There aren't any trucks	**on**	the bridge.
There's an office building	**between**	the store **and** the restaurant.
Are there any cars	**on**	the bridge?
What is	**between**	the lake **and** the house?

Look at this view! There are some clouds _____ the sky _____ the mountains. There is a river _____ those two hills that goes _____ a lake. There are some ducks _____ the lake. Let's give them some bread!

If you finish an activity in this unit before your classmates, try one of these.

A Do the crossword puzzle.

Across

4. Please buy a loaf of b_____d to make sandwiches.

5. I only drink soda if it's in a b_____e.

6. I dropped an e_____g and broke it.

7. I drink two c_____s of soda every day.

Down

1. Americans eat baked p_____s with sour cream.

2. I can't open this j_____r of pickles. The top is on too tight.

3. I don't like the smell of g_____c.

5. I sometimes eat cereal right out of the b_____x.

B Talk with a partner about food.

1. What's your favorite fruit?

2. What's your favorite vegetable?

3. What's your favorite meat?

4. Are there any fruits, vegetables, or meats you don't like?

C Look at the chart. Then finish the dialog with *some*, *any*, *much*, or *many*.

Level **Up** ▶ *Some, Any, Much, Many*	
Is there **any** ice cream?	Yes, there's **some** in the refrigerator. No, we don't have **any**. Yes, but there isn't **much**.
Are there **any** apples?	Yes, we have **some**, but not **many**. No, we don't have **any**.
Can I have **some** water?	Yes. Here's **some** water for you.

A: We have _____ cherries at home, but not _____.

B: Are there _____ cherries in this store?

A: No, but there are _____ strawberries.

B: Strawberries? OK, let's buy _____ for dessert.

A: We don't have _____ sugar either.

B: Really? Let's buy _____ of that too.

If you finish an activity in this unit before your classmates, try one of these.

A Do the crossword puzzle about special holidays in the United States.

Across

1. We usually have a party at midnight on
   N_____ _____'s Eve.
4. Santa Claus comes on C_____s Eve.
5. Children wear costumes on H_____n.
7. In the U.S. and Canada, people eat turkey
   and give thanks on T_____g Day.
8. I usually take my mom to dinner on
   M_____'s Day.

Down

2. People play tricks on each other on
   A____l Fool's Day.
3. I sometimes get chocolate on
   V_____'s Day.
6. I always take my dad to a baseball game on F_____'s Day.

B Talk about family traditions with a partner.

1. Are there special days when your family gets together?
2. Do you have any family traditions on holidays?
3. Are there special foods that you eat on holidays?
4. Where does your family go on holidays?

C Look at the chart. Then use *in*, *on*, or *at* to complete the paragraph.

> **Level Up ▶** *In, On, At*
>
> I usually sleep late **in** the summer. I get up **at** 9.
> I often play a trick on my sister **on** April Fool's Day.
> I sometimes buy fruit **at** the Farmer's Festival.

Chinese New Year begins _____ the first day of the first lunar month of the year. In the Western calendar, it starts _____ January or _____ February. _____ the day before Chinese New Year—New Year's Eve—families get together _____ about 6 p.m. and have dinner parties.

If you finish an activity in this unit before your classmates, try one of these.

A Say each of these tongue twisters quickly three times.

1. The cook cooked a cake.
2. Six sick students.
3. The teacher's peach speech.
4. Sad staff's laugh.

B Talk with a partner about being a helpful person.

1. Do you ever cook or clean for someone else?
2. Do you help anyone study or do their job?
3. Is there anyone with a problem whom you talk to sometimes?
4. Do you ever take care of any children? Who? How?

C Look at the chart. Then use the hints to write *Do you mean . . .* questions.

Level **Up** ▶ *Do you mean . . . ?*	
He works in the office.	**Do you mean** the main office? **Do you mean** the office near the entrance? **Do you mean** the man who sits by the door?

1. John is a teacher.   _____ English teacher?
2. He works in a nearby restaurant. _____ near the school?
3. I like the security guard.   _____ at the entrance?
4. She drives everyday.   _____ to work?

If you finish an activity in this unit before your classmates, try one of these.

A Do the word search. Find nine names of jobs or professions.

cook
doctor
driver
engineer
farmer
manager
nurse
teacher
waiter

d	k	o	o	c	m	r	k	c	o
o	n	u	r	s	e	k	r	a	r
c	e	m	r	h	v	e	e	e	r
t	h	d	c	w	g	r	l	m	e
o	e	a	r	a	s	r	c	r	e
r	e	e	n	i	g	n	e	b	m
t	e	a	k	t	v	e	e	i	n
e	m	a	r	e	a	e	a	p	e
s	c	f	a	r	m	e	r	s	s
i	e	m	r	o	v	a	l	e	z
a	e	v	y	k	j	e	e	u	q

B Talk with a partner about jobs.

1. Do you have a job?

2. What are three things you have to do?

3. What do you like about your job?

4. What do you dislike about it?

C Look at the chart. Then write two more sentences about what a bus driver should do.

> **Level Up ▶** *Should*
>
> *Should* is used for something that is important or a good idea to do.
>
> You **should** smile at customers.
> You **should** say, "Come again" when customers leave.

1. You should be friendly to the people who ride on your bus.

2. You should take a break if you feel tired.

3. _____

4. _____

When You Have Time ▶ Extra Activities: Unit 8

If you finish an activity in this unit before your classmates, try one of these.

A Two doctors in Jakarta meet in the street and start talking to each other. Both are married. Neither is divorced. One is the father of the other's son. How can this be? Who are they? See the answer at the bottom of this page.

B Talk with a partner about your family.

1. Who raised you?

2. Who do you live with now?

3. Which members of your family are you closest to?

4. Who are your favorite relatives? Why?

C Look at the chart. Then write the questions for these answers.

Level Up ▶ Talking About Ancestors	
Where **was** he **born**?	He **was born** in Austria.
When **did** she **get married**?	She **got married** in 1978.
What **were** her children's names?	Her children's names **were** Jon and Sue.

1. _____ He grew up in Germany.

2. _____ His parents' names were Jan and Helga.

3. _____ He lived in a small house.

4. _____ He was born in 1980.

5. _____ He got married in London.

Answer to activity A riddle: The doctors are husband and wife.

When You Have Time **119**

If you finish an activity in this unit before your classmates, try one of these.

A Do the word search. Find the past tense of these verbs.

play	ride	go
study	see	buy
meet	find	take

a	b	s	r	o	g	i	f	s	t
f	d	e	y	a	l	p	u	t	s
t	e	m	o	t	d	w	n	h	y
e	i	e	r	o	d	e	n	u	a
p	d	t	k	b	n	n	i	n	i
m	u	a	e	o	u	t	p	k	o
a	t	h	g	u	o	b	d	r	p
n	s	i	w	e	f	t	e	s	w
i	e	m	r	o	v	a	l	a	r
l	d	d	i	r	s	t	s	a	q

B Talk with a partner about personal experiences.

1. What was the scariest thing you ever saw?

2. Who was the most famous person you ever met?

3. What was the most embarrassing thing you ever did?

4. What was the most expensive thing you ever bought?

C Look at the chart. Then unscramble and write sentences.

> **Level Up ▶ Past Verbs with Infinitives**
>
> I **wanted to pass** the test. I **had to study**.
> I **forgot to bring** my book home. I **started to cry**.

1. (a car / to buy / I / wanted / I was in high school / when)

_____

2. (to save / last year / some money / I tried)

_____

3. (French / speak / to / in Paris / learned / I)

_____

4. (when / I didn't like / early / wake up / to / I was a child)

_____

If you finish an activity in this unit before your classmates, try one of these.

A Do the Famous Sites Quiz. Match the pictures and names.

1. Colosseum, Rome   **3.** Taj Mahal, Agra   **5.** Golden Gate Bridge, San Francisco

2. Big Ben, London   **4.** Eiffel Tower, Paris   **6.** Wat Arun, Bangkok

B Talk about travel with a partner.

1. Tell me about an interesting trip you took.

2. Where do you want to visit someday?

3. What kind of tour do you want to take?

4. If a friend comes to visit from another country, where is a good place to take that friend?

C Look at the chart. *Will* and *going to* are both ways to talk about the future, but use *going to* to talk about plans you've already made. Rewrite the sentences below with *going to*.

> **Level Up ▸** *Going to . . .*
>
> **I'm going to go** shopping later.
> My brother and I **are going to buy** a new computer.
> We **are not going to get** a printer. We already have one.

1. My brother will go to Hong Kong tomorrow. _____

2. My family will take him to the airport. _____

3. I'll call him tomorrow to make sure he's OK. _____

4. My sister and I will visit him next week, but we won't stay in his apartment. _____

If you finish an activity in this unit before your classmates, try one of these.

A Do the Famous 20th Century Romances Quiz. Match the pictures and sentences.

1. Hillary and Bill Clinton have both worked in U.S. politics.

2. Barbie and Ken made a doll company rich.

3. Bonnie and Clyde were bank robbers.

4. Mickey and Minnie were TV stars.

5. John Lennon was a member of the Beatles, and Yoko Ono was his Japanese wife.

B Talk about your friends with a partner.

1. Who are your two or three best friends?

2. What are they like?

3. What do you like to do together?

4. When do you meet?

C Look at the chart. Then rewrite the sentences below with *that*.

Level Up ▶ *That* Instead of *Who*

I want to meet someone **who** likes children.	I want to meet someone **that** likes children.
I want to meet someone **who** I can trust.	I want to meet someone **that** I can trust.

1. I want a partner who isn't shy. _____

2. I like people who are good at singing. _____

3. I want a partner who likes going to clubs. _____

4. I don't like people who get angry a lot. _____

If you finish an activity in this unit before your classmates, try one of these.

A Do the American Sign Language Quiz. Number the pictures to show the order of these words. (Hint: the fingers look like letters.)

I-L-Y (for "I love you")

B Talk with a partner about things you're good at.

1. Can you dance, draw, sing, or play an instrument?

2. Did you ever study any of these things?

3. Can you imitate anyone famous?

4. Can you tell any jokes in English?

C Look at the chart. Then complete the explanation about how to juggle three balls.

> **Level Up ▶ Describing Multiple Actions**
>
> Push these two buttons **at the same time**.
> Hold this button down, **while** mov**ing** the mouse.
> **Keep** typ**ing** and push**ing** buttons.

Here's how to juggle three balls.

1. Hold one ball in your left hand and two balls in your right hand.

2. Throw one of the balls in your right hand.

3. Catch the ball with your left hand, _____

_____ing the other ball.

4. Keep _____ balls in the air and

_____ them.

Top 50 Irregular Verbs

This is an irregular verb list. The verbs in this list are arranged by how frequently they are used, with 1 being the most frequent.

Rank	Base Form	Past Tense Form	Past Participle
1	say	said	said
2	make	made	made
3	go	went	gone
4	take	took	taken
5	come	came	come
6	see	saw	seen
7	know	knew	known
8	get	got	got/gotten (U.S.)
9	give	gave	given
10	find	found	found
11	think	thought	thought
12	tell	told	told
13	become	became	become
14	show	showed	shown
15	leave	left	left
16	feel	felt	felt
17	put	put	put
18	bring	brought	brought
19	begin	began	begun
20	keep	kept	kept
21	hold	held	held
22	write	wrote	written
23	stand	stood	stood
24	hear	heard	heard
25	let	let	let

Rank	Base Form	Past Tense Form	Past Participle
26	mean	meant	meant
27	set	set	set
28	meet	met	met
29	run	ran	run
30	pay	paid	paid
31	sit	sat	sat
32	speak	spoke	spoken
33	lie	lay	lain
34	lead	led	led
35	read	read	read
36	grow	grew	grown
37	lose	lost	lost
38	fall	fell	fallen
39	send	sent	sent
40	build	built	built
41	understand	understood	understood
42	draw	drew	drawn
43	break	broke	broken
44	spend	spent	spent
45	cut	cut	cut
46	rise	rose	risen
47	drive	drove	driven
48	buy	bought	bought
49	wear	wore	worn
50	choose	chose	chosen